The History
of the
Newport City Flag

James Alan Egan
Newport Tower Museum
152 Mill Street
Newport, Rhode Island
02840

ISBN-13: 978-1500887056

ISBN-10: 1500887056

James Alan Egan
curator of the
Newport Tower Museum
152 Mill Street
Newport, RI 02840

published by
Cosmopolite Press
152 Mill Street
Newport RI, 02840

Printed in the United States of America

Dedicated to Brian Sullivan and Peter Tyler,
who have enthusiastically led the effort to
revive the use of the Newport City Flag.

Special thanks to:

Gladys E. Bolhouse, Curator of Manuscripts of the Newport Historical Society from 1946 to 1992,
Whitney Pape and Robert Kelly of the Special Collections Department of the Redwood Library,
The Reference Department staff at the Newport Public Library,
Bert Lippincott, Newport Historical Society Librarian,
Rosemary Watt, of the Glasgow Museum in Scotland,
and Patrick F. Murphy, Newport City Historian.

TABLE OF CONTENTS

AMOR VINCET OMNIA

INTRODUCTION

The Roaring Twenties was a time of wealth and prosperity in America.
But in 1929 and 1930, when Newport was adopting its official city
flag, the decade of excess was about to come to a roaring halt.

In the spring of 1929, Newport held the second of two
city-wide contests for the design of an official flag.

In August, 1930 the winner was chosen and the Newport Flag
Committee presented its report to the Board of Aldermen.

October 29, 1929 was Black Tuesday.
Stock markets in the US and around the globe crashed,
leading to the Great Depression, which lingered for a decade.

The winter of 1929 must have been long and cold for the
wealthy of Newport, as they watched their fortunes dwindle.

But in April, as the daffodils were blooming, the
Aldermen approved the design of the Newport City Flag
(with a few minor alterations).

When summer arrived, Newport fully blossomed, because
the eyes of the world were focused on the City by the Sea.
The British were coming. No, not the Redcoats.
They had occupied Newport during the Revolutionary War.
These new Brits were here to challenge the Americans in another way.

But before we find out how, let's review the details of the
well-thought-out process by which Newport adopted its city flag.

In 1928, the first Newport City Flag contest produced lukewarm results

The FIRST Newport City Flag Contest was held during the spring of 1928:

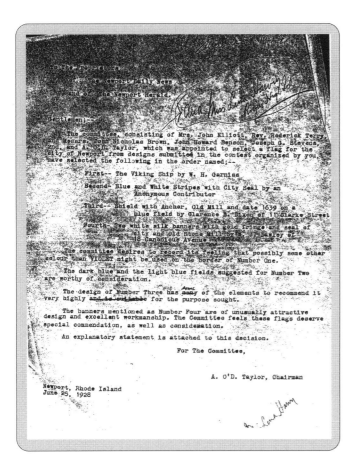

To The Proprietors of
The Newport Daily News
and of The Newport Herald

Gentlemen;--

The committee, consisting of
Mrs. John Elliott, Miss Lena Harvey
(from Rogers High School), Rev.
Roderick Terry, Messrs. John Nicholas
Brown, John Howard Benson, Joseph
G. Stevens, 2nd, and A. O'D. Taylor,
which was appointed to select the flag
for the city of Newport from designs
submitted in the contest organized by
you, have selected the following in the
order named;--

First -- The Viking Ship by W. H. Garniss

Second -- Blue and White Stripes with City Seal by an Anonymous Contributor

Third-- Shield with Anchor, Old Mill and date 1639 on a blue field by Clarence B. Dixon of 11 Clarke St.

Fourth-- two white silk banners with gold fringe and seal of city and Old Stone Mill by W. J. Dawley of 18 Canonicus Avenue.

The committee declares to record its feeling that possibly some other color than Violet might be used on the border of Number One.

The dark blue and light blue fields suggested for Number Two are worthy of consideration.

The design of Number Three has some of the elements to recommend it very highly for the purpose sought.

The banners mentioned as Number Four are of unusually attractive design and excellent workmanship.

The Committee feels these flags deserve special commendation, as well as consideration.

An explanatory statement is attached to this decision.

For The Committee,

A. O' D. Taylor, Chairman

Newport, Rhode Island,
June 25, 1928

Reading between the lines, it appears to me that the Flag Committee wasn't crazy about any of the designs. To be polite, they found something nice to say about each one. They all deserve special "commendation," but really only "consideration." They didn't really pick a winner. Not even the Viking ship on violet.

A YEAR LATER, IN 1929, THE SECOND FLAG CONTEST WAS HELD

Newport Daily News
Wednesday, June 19, 1929

FLAG DESIGNS SOUGHT.

Suitable Emblem to
Represent City of Newport

Appeal to Artists and Designers is
Continuance of Request Made by
Aldermen and Mayor

To the Editor of the News:
The members of the city flag committee desire to again appeal to the artists and designers of the city and County of Newport to send in their designs for a suitable flag to be selected to represent the city of Newport. This is in continuance of the request made by the Board of Aldermen and the mayor of Newport.

These suggestions, which were made at the meeting at the Art Association on this subject, are recognized as having been of great value. And coming as they did from Captain McCandless, the nationally recognized expert on such matters, they should prove doubly valuable to all competitors. Attention was drawn in the public press to this talk and all artists were advised to attend. The central idea was given as "liberty" and the historical incidents arising around this subject were explained. Religious Liberty, Sons of Liberty, Liberty Tree, etc. were spoken of.

In order to push this project forward, the following instructions and suggestions are now given.

It is suggested that:
1— First prize for the successful designer shall be $100
2— Second prize for the second best design shall be $25
3— All designs must be on white paper of the size 36 inches by 24 inches
4— A margin of not over 6 inches may surround the design.
5— Design should be in actual colors suggested and not over five colors in all.

6— No actually made flag should be submitted

7— Designs should be suitable for a printed flag or sewn bunting.

8— No competitor who has entered a design will be permitted to act on the judges' committee of award.

9— All designs must be delivered to the city clerk's office, at City Hall, marked "City Flag Committee" on or before July 30, 1929.

10— Competitors must write their names and addresses on the reverse side of the paper carrying design.

11— Two sheets of paper must be used if the design differs on each side of the flag.

12— All residents of Newport County are eligible as competitors, and no entrance fee is required.

This information is given now in the hope that the entire list of designers and artists will find time to present their designs to by July 30.

For City Flag Committee.
A O'D Taylor,
Chairman

The Flag Committee has gotten professional advice and has clarified the parameters of the contest. And they promised $100 for the winner. Adjusting for inflation, $100 in 1929 would be about $1350 today.

FLAG SUGGESTIONS

On Saturday, July 27, 1929 the Newport Daily News published some "Flag Suggestions" submitted by A. O'D. Taylor, chairman of the Newport City Flag Committee.

(The article had no illustrations, but I have added some to clarify the text.)

Incidentally, the Seal of the City of Newport mentioned in this newspaper article features a circular engraving of the Newport skyline as seen looking towards the east from Narragansett Bay.

In the foreground is the lighthouse at the northern end of Goat Island. Beyond are some boats in Newport Harbor as well as several prominent buildings and church spires.

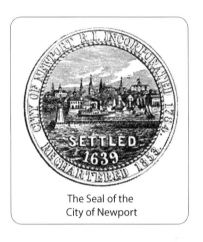

The Seal of the
City of Newport

*Newport Daily News
Saturday, July 27, 1929*

FLAG SUGGESTIONS.

The recent discovery of the old Newport seal adds a new interest in the search for an appropriate civic device for a Newport city flag, which is again being discussed.

Of course, the ideal civic device or emblem should be heraldic in character and so conform to all the requirements of distinguishability and artistic effect. The ideal device should, if possible, be some easily remembered and easily recognizable design, based, if practical, on something significant or symbolic of the city that it represents. If the device is thus chosen, it can be treated heraldically and placed on a shield in appropriate colors arranged according to the time-honored heraldic rules which, by the way, are also in the best artistic taste.

Such a coat-of-arms for a city may then serve as a basis for the design of the city seal and of the city flag. For the city seal, the coat-of-arms can be placed in a circle and surrounded by an appropriate inscription. For the city flag, the device of the arms should be used without the shield, but with the field color of the shield as the field color of the flag.

Such use of the civic coat-of-arms as the basis of the civic seal and civic flag is in accordance with the very best usage in America, in the British Isles and in Continental Europe. It is the culmination of the gradual usage developed through centuries. Violations of these general rules will of course be found, especially in devices adopted during the Victorian period, which was particularly decadent in such matters. There is a growing tendency among American cities that adopted devices in the nineteenth century, to bring their device more in accordance with the generally accepted standards. At present the flags of several of our cities violate not only the principles of heraldry and art but likewise those of distinguishability. When a new city flag is to be adopted, advantage should be taken of the opportunity to design something in the very best possible taste.

A seal, as such, should never appear upon a flag, but the salient device of the seal, without any of the inscription or other accessories, that are sometimes necessary on a seal, should appear. The flag of the Common Council of Providence is a fine example of good taste in this respect.

Such use of the civic coat-of-arms as the basis of the civic seal and civic flag is in accordance with the very best usage in America, in the British Isles, and in continental Europe. It is the culmination of the gradual usage developed through centuries. Violations of these general rules will of course be found especially in devices adopted during the Victorian period, which was particularly decadent in such matters.

There is a growing tendency among American cities that adopted devices in the nineteenth century to bring their device more in accordance with the generally accepted standards. At present, the flags of several of our cities violate not only the principles of heraldry and art, but likewise those of distinguishability. When a new city flag is adopted, advantage should be taken of the opportunity to design something in the very best possible taste.

A seal, as such, should never appear upon a flag, but the salient device of the seal, without any of the inscription or other accessories, that are sometimes necessary on a seal, should appear. The flag of the Common Council of Providence is a fine example of good taste in this respect.

The arms of a city should never appear as arms on a flag; that is, the shield itself should not appear on the flag, but only the device on the shield.

Seal of the Common Council of Providence

Flag of the Common Council of Providence

The arms, flag and seal of the United States are good example of this and indeed a good example of the whole subject. The coat-of-arms of the United States is thirteen stripes, white and red, with a blue band at the top of the shield heraldically "Paleways [vertically]of thirteen pieces argent and gules [silver (or white) and red], a chief azure [top part is blue]."

This coat-of-arms appears as the main device of the seal of the United States and also without the shield, as the main device of the United States flag, with three slight modifications, a reduction in the size of the blue part, and an addition of the stars.

Shield of the coat-of-arms of the United States

Great Seal of the United States

Flag of the United States

The flag of Harvard University has recently been changed, from a flag bearing the arms of the university on the shield to a flag on which the device of the arms appears without any shield, a red flag with three white books.

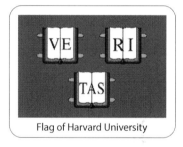

Flag of Harvard University

Flag of Massachusetts

(reverse side)

The Massachusetts state flag is a terrible example of a violation of this rule. The Rhode Island flag is a step up in the right direction, but still has room for improvement.

[By "room for improvement," A. O'D. Taylor might be suggesting that, according to the strict rules of heraldry, a gold symbol, like the stars and anchor on the RI Flag, should not be placed on a silver or white background.]

Flag of Rhode Island

One of the tentative designs for a Newport coat-of-arms recently suggested is "Quarterly, a ship, the Old Stone Mill, a torpedo, and a sheep.

As a general rule a quartered coat is not the best design for a city's arms. In the first place, quartering has a special use and meaning in heraldry and only under peculiar circumstances would it be particularly apt for a city.

The sheep has an historical value as an old Newport emblem or device. The sheep, adopted as a device by Newport as early as 1729, is one of the earliest of American civic devices and on that account might well be retained by the city. The Old Stone Mill has an historical and sentimental value and at the same time is particularly significant and symbolic of Newport. It would readily be recognized as significant of Newport. It is probably the oldest building in New England today.

The Old Stone Mill by itself as a silver medal on a green field, heraldically "Vert, a mill argent" would be very effective and significant coat-of-arms for the city. It could be used as the chief device of the city seal which is now an atrocious Victorian type of seal, a view of the city, evidently inspired by the equally atrocious seal of Boston with a view of that city.

The arms as described above could be placed effectively on the flag as a green flag bearing the Old Stone Mill in white. This would be simple and easy to recognize. If a more complicated coat-of-arms is desired, a chief [the top part of the shield], charged with the historic sheep, might be added. Vert, a mill argent, on a chief or a sheep sable (A black sheep on gold).

[In other words, a silver or white Old Stone Mill, on a green shield, the top part of which is gold with a black sheep.]

Seal of the City of Boston

Raising the money for the prizes

On the same day, another article appeared, politely soliciting the $75.00 more needed for the Flag Contest prizes:

Newport Daily News
Saturday, July 27, 1929

NEWPORT'S CITY FLAG FUND NEARLY RAISED

It is expected that the small amount still necessary for the prize money for the designs sent in to the Competition for a City Flag for Newport will be subscribed during this week. Only $75 is required to meet the expenses. Among the dozen artistic designs received by the committee, it is believed that several will be found worthy of representing the city.

Owing to the absence of two members of the committee in the Europe, Mr. John Nicholas Brown and Mr. J Howard Benson, two substitutes Mr. William H. Cotton and Miss Louise Sturtevant have been asked to act, and have accepted the honor. News of the award will be made as early as possible.

THE WINNER IS ANNOUNCED

Newport Herald
August 10, 1929

JOHN L. SMITH IS WINNER OF FLAG CONTEST

The selection of the best design submitted for a flag to represent the city and to be known as the "Newport City Flag" was made yesterday afternoon by the City Flag committee. This Committee consisting of Mrs. Maud Howe Elliott, Rev. Roderick Terry, Miss Mary E. Harvey, Messrs. John Nicholas Brown, J. Howard Benson, Joseph G. Stevens and A. O'D. Taylor as chairman.

Miss Harvey, Mr. Brown, and Mr. Benson, being absent from the city, their places were graciously and ably filled by Miss Louise Sturtevant, Miss Virginia Braman and Mr. William H. Cotton.

All of the seven members were present yesterday, and after long and careful consideration awarded the first prize of $100 to Mr. John L. Smith of 24 Almy Street and the second prize of $25 to Miss Marjorie Wilson of 51 Dresser St.

The design of the first-prize winner is a most simple and clear one. It is a flag with a white field in the center of which is a plainly sketched picture of the Old Stone Mill. Outside of this is a formal wreath of green leaves and below in a blue ribbon on which the word Newport appears in gold. There is a gold fringe border on the outside border of the flag.

[Generally, gold fringe is a decorative adornment
and is only used on flags displayed indoors.
Fringe is omitted for flags flown outdoors
as it frays when whipped by the wind.]

My conjectured illustration of
Miss Marjorie Wilson's design for the Newport
City Flag, which won the "second prize"

The design for the second-prize winner's contribution is more complicated. It also is a white field flag with a Shield in red and yellow quartering, on which appears the emblems of the Old Stone Mill, the Liberty Tree, the Constellation [a Navy sloop-of-war built in 1854], and the Memorial Tower [in Miantonomi Park]. A black scroll runs over the shield on which is printed "Liberty, Peace, Independence." The whole design is masked and most effective.

Other excellent designs were laid before the committee and the entire exhibition was excellent. Much conscientious work had been put into each.

Mrs. Emily Burling Manchester had an Old Stone Mill design on a white field with green trees behind. Mr. John L Smith had a striking design of an old Viking Ship coming head-on before a "big blow" and the word Newport.

John Stevens had an interesting historical design of Red and White perpendicular stripes representing the old R. I. Revolutionary flag with white center and a green "Liberty Tree," around which is coiled a rattlesnake and the word "Beware," also the word "Newport R. I.," an indicative emblem of the city's historic insistence on Liberty.

Mrs. Anita B. Chase had a design of the Old Fort, the Constellation, Old Mill, and Memorial Tower, with the word "Newport R. I."

Mrs. J. B. Edward submitted a rather striking flag of brilliant blue with a fine gold seal of the city in the centre.

Mr. William Garniss had a delicately traced design in Blue and White, including a Sea Gull, a Viking Ship, the Old Stone Mill, an outline of Aquidneck and the words "Rhode, Newport Island."

Miss Wilson, the designer of the second prize exhibit also had two other most excellent designs, which included the emblems which appear on her prize-winning design, but included the Viking ravens in black. All these exhibits were remarkable for the excellence of the workmanship and it was difficult to decide which was the best. Suitability for the purposes of a flag came largely under consideration.

The committee expressed the opinion that their decision was made of the designs laid before them and future committees should consider adapting these designs for the purpose desired.

Their conclusions were unanimous and made after weighing all sides of the many questions which came up. The decision to award these prizes as indicated, leaves to the city authorities or other committees the full free right to accept or reject any or all the designs for city purposes.

The great importance of actually obtaining the very best design for the flag for a "Newport City Flag" is a difficult one to be assured of.

Mr. J. H. Barney of Barney's Music Store has volunteered to place all the designs received in his large show window at 140 Thames Street this morning so the public may see all of the flag designs which appeared in this competition. They will be there till Sunday; it is hoped the balance of the expense which the effort necessitated will be subscribed when people see what has been done.

My conjectured illustration of the
Flag Committee presenting the prize
winners to the Board of Aldermen,
on Friday, August 16, 1929

NEWPORT HERALD. SATURDAY AUGUST 10, 1929.

DESIGN FOR PROPOSED CITY FLAG.

The Herald shows here, as well as the facilities of a newspaper can, the best design for a Newport city flag. It has been selected by a committee of which Mr. A. O'D Taylor is president, and it is understood that they will recommend to the mayor and board of aldermen that they accept it is an official ensign of the

unicipaplity. As stated yesterday the design is by Mr. John L. Smith of 24 Almy street. Mr. Smith is a mason by trade and works at it daily, but he dabbles in art and that too very successfully, as may be seen.

But a newspaper cut can not begin to do justice to Mr Smith's work as the coloring is a fine feature and

colors can not yet be reproduced in a newspaper cut. For instance the fringe of the flag is of gold and in the cut it appears black. The wreath is green and the ribbon below it is blue. They naturally appear black in the cut. Moreover the word Newport is gold.

The cut, however gives a very clear idea of the motive and the design.

Newport Herald,
Saturday August 10 1929

DESIGN FOR PROPOSED CITY FLAG

The Herald shows here, as well as the facilities of a newspaper can, the best design for a Newport city flag. It has been selected by a committee of which Mr. A. O'D Taylor is president, and it is understood that they will recommend to the mayor and board of aldermen that they accept it as an official ensign of the municipality. As stated yesterday the design is by John L. Smith of 24 Almy Street. Mr. Smith is a mason by trade and works at it daily, but he dabbles in art and that too very successfully, as may be seen.

But a newspaper cut can not begin to do justice to Mr. Smith's work as the coloring is a fine feature and colors can not yet be reproduced in a newspaper cut. For instance the fringe of the flag is of gold and in the cut it appears black. The wreath is green and the ribbon below it is blue. They naturally appear black in the cut. Moreover the word Newport is in gold.

The cut, however gives a very clear idea of the motive and the design.

Even the Providence Journal carried the story
of the new Newport City Flag

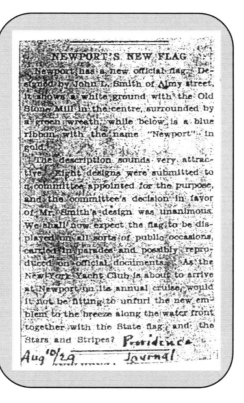

Providence Journal
August 10, 1929

NEWPORT'S NEW FLAG

Newport has a new official flag. Designed by John L. Smith of Almy Street, it shows a white ground with Old Stone Mill in the center, surrounded by a green wreath, while below is a blue ribbon with the name "Newport" in gold.

The description sounds very attractive. Eight designs were submitted to a committee appointed for the purpose and the committee's decision in favor of Mr. Smith's design was unanimous. We shall now expect the flag to be displayed on all sorts of public occasions, carried in parades, and possibly reproduced on official documents.

As the New York Yacht Club is about to arrive at Newport on its annual cruise, would it not be fitting to unfurl the new emblem to the breeze along the waterfront together with the State flag and the Stars & Stripes?

THE PROMINENT NEWPORTERS ON THE FLAG COMMITTEE

The Chairman of the committee, **Alexander O'D. Taylor** (1883-1962) was a Newport businessman who wrote a book on the history of Jamestown.

His father, Alexander O'Driscoll Taylor Sr. (1832-1910) had emigrated from Cork, Ireland in 1883. Taylor Sr. first worked with the U.S. Geological Survey with the famous Newport geographer Raphael Pumpelly, then later became a Newport realtor, and helped develop Jamestown as a summer colony.

Alexander O'D. Taylor Jr.'s son, Erich O'D. Taylor was a State Senator from Newport in the 1970s who was instrumental in the cleanup of Fort Adams.

Maud Howe Elliot
(1854-1948)

Maud Howe Elliott (1854-1948) was the author of twenty books. Her mother was Julia Ward Howe, who wrote the lyrics to the "Battle Hymn of the Republic."

Maud's father was Samuel Grindley Howe, founder and first director of the Perkins School for the Blind in Boston.

After marrying the English artist John Elliott in 1887, Maud lived in Italy for a dozen or so years before moving to Newport.

She became a patron of the arts and was a founding member of the Newport Art Association. She was also the founder of the Progressive Party and played an active role in the suffragette movement.

With her sister, Laura Elliott Richards, Maud wrote a biography of their mother, *The Life of Julia Ward Howe*, which won a Pulitzer Prize. Maud also wrote a *Newport Aquarelle* (a fancy name for "*Watercolor*") and *This Was My Newport*, which was published in 1994, when she was 90 years old.

Maud served on the Miantonomi Park Memorial Commission, which constructed the World War I Memorial Tower in 1929.

The Library of the Late
Rev. Dr. Roderick Terry

Rev. Dr. Roderick Terry served as the minister of the South Reformed Church in New York City for many years. After retiring, he moved to Newport. In 1929, he was 80 years old.

A 3-volume set of memorabilia and correspondence with his many notable friends was published after he died.

Miss Mary E. Harvey was an art teacher for many years in the Townsend Industrial School, at 39 Broadway, which, in the twentieth century, evolved into the Thompson Middle School.

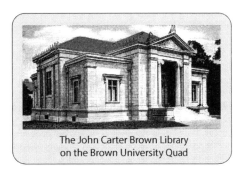

The John Carter Brown Library
on the Brown University Quad

John Nicholas Brown 2nd came from a long line of distinguished antiquarians.

His grandfather, John Carter Brown (1797-1874), had a library collection so extensive that his son, John Nicholas Brown 1st (1561-1900), built a library to house it. The John Carter Brown Library, a charming classical building, still graces the quad at Brown University.

John Nicholas Brown 2nd (1900-1979) was only two months old when his father died of typhoid fever. The father's brother, Harold Brown was in Italy, but took the first boat home for the funeral. Unfortunately, the stress of brother's death was too much, and Harold also died. At the age of three months, John Nicholas Brown 2nd had inherited his family's fortune. The media dubbed him "the richest baby in America."

In 1922, he graduated Magna Cum Laude from Harvard in the History and Literature of Classical Cultures. After World War II, he became the Special Cultural Advisor for the Monuments, Fine Arts, and Archives program (MFAA) helping to supervise the return of art treasures stolen by the Nazis to their rightful owners. (The work of the MFAA was recently depicted in the movie *The Monuments Men*.) He later went on to become the United States Assistant Secretary of the Navy under President Harry Truman from 1946 to 1949.

John Nicholas Brown 2nd donated the Providence Public Library in Providence and the ornate chapel at St. George's School in Middletown. He helped rehabilitate old Brick Market house in Newport, the Arcade building in Providence and the Slater Mill in Pawtucket. After he died, his widow donated the funds to build the Emmanuel Episcopal Church in Newport. The Brown's summer estate overlooking Newport Harbor was acquired by the New York Yacht Club in 1987.

John Nicholas Brown 2nd

John Howard Benson
(1901-1956)

John Howard Benson (1901-1956) was a famous stone carver, calligrapher, and teacher at RISD. Along with Arthur Graham Carey, he was the author of *The Elements of Lettering*. His son, John Everett "Fud" Benson, and grandson, Nicholas Waite Benson operate The John Stevens Shop, one of the oldest continuously operating businesses in the United States. John Stevens opened the stone carving shop on upper Thames Street in 1705. In 1927, after the Stevens family had run the shop for more than 220 years, it was purchased by John Howard Benson.

Joseph G. Stevens 2nd was an architect who put an addition on the back of George Chaplin Mason's Newport Historical Society building on Touro Street. To ensure it was fireproof, he designed it with steel beams and brick walls. The Stevens family came to Newport in the early 1700's. Thomas Stevens was a famous cutler, who manufactured knives for many of the fishermen in Newport, Cape Cod, and the Islands. (In the wintertime, he manufactured skates.)

Ms. Louise Sturtevant attended Wellesley College and the Medical School of Boston. She and her sister Helena were both talented painters and founding artist members of the Art Association of Newport, which purchased the John N. A. Griswold House in 1915 and created the Newport Art Museum.

The colorful Newport scenes that still grace the corridors of Newport City Hall were painted by Louise's sister, Helena Sturtevant.

Virginia Hall Braman was born in New Haven, Connecticut, later moved to Newport, and lived until she was 93.

William Henry "Will" Cotton (1880-1958) was a caricaturist, a portrait painter, and a playwright. He produced illustrations for the *New Yorker* and produced a comedy show on Broadway. He painted mural decorations including those in the Apollo Theater, the Times Square Theater, and the old pavilion at Easton's Beach.

He was a descendent of the colonial Puritan minister John Cotton. Will's father and grandfather were prominent medical practitioners in Newport for many years.

William Henry "Will" Cotton
(1880-1958)

THE FLAG COMMITTEE'S REPORT TO THE ALDERMEN

Newport Daily News
Friday, August 16, 1929

PRIZES AWARDED

Report of Flag Committee Approved
at Aldermanic Meeting

If the Representative Council follows the action taken by the Board of Aldermen at its weekly meeting Thursday evening, the city will have an official flag.

The Aldermen approved the report of the flag committee, of which Mr. A. O' D. Taylor was chairman, and referred the report and the winning flag designs to the Representative Council, for such action as it deems best.

Mr. John L. Smith and Miss Marjorie Wilson, winners of the first and second prizes were present and received from Mrs. Maud Howe Elliott checks for $100 and $25, respectively.

PRIZES AWARDED

Report of Flag Committee Approved at Aldermanic Meeting

If the Representative Council follows the action taken by the Board of Aldermen at its weekly meeting Thursday evening, the city will have an official flag. The aldermen approved the report of the flag committee, of which Mr. A. O.'D. Taylor was chairman, and referred the report and the winning flag designs to the Representative Council, for such action as it deems best. Mr. John L. Smith and Miss Marjorie Wilson, winners of the first and second prizes, were present and received from Mrs. Maud Howe Elliott checks for $100 and $25, respectively.

Following is the flag report read by Mr. Taylor:

"The committee appointed by you to secure a suitable design for Municipal Flag, to represent the city of Newport, and which committee consists of Mrs. Maud Howe Elliott, Rev Roderick Terry, Miss Mary E. Harvey, Mr. John Nicholas Brown, Mr. Joseph G. Stevens, 2nd, Mr. John Howard Benson and Mr. A. O'D. Taylor, begs to report:

1st. That they have given time and thought to this matter, and have aimed to secure the best advice on the subject from artists, designers and others.

2nd, Captain Byron McCandless, U. S. N., the national authority on flags was consulted by your committee and met with them on this subject. He later spoke publicly giving his views as to what a City Flag should be.

3rd, Your committee spread abroad the ideas gained, and offered two prizes, one of $100 and the other of $25, for the most suitable design that might be suggested by designers.

4th, The competition was open to all artists, designers or other persons of Newport county.

5th, The prize money was secured through voluntary public subscription, the appeal being sanctioned by His Honor, Mayor Mortimer A. Sullivan.

6th, On Thursday, August 8, 1929 your committee met in the office of the board of canvassers and made their selections from the designs submitted.

7th. Owing to the absence from the city of Mr. Brown, Mr. Benson and Miss Harvey, their places on the committee were filled by Mr. William Cotton, Miss Louise Sturtevant and Miss Virginia Braman who with Mrs. Elliott, Rev. Dr. Terry, Mr. Stevens and Mr. Taylor formed the acting selective committee.

8th. The first prize was awarded to the design of the Old Stone Mill with a wreath of green leaves, and a blue scroll with "Newport" in gold letters, on a white field, surrounded by gold fringe. It was submitted by Mr. John L. Smith.

Following is the flag report read by Mr. Taylor:

The committee appointed by you to secure a suitable design for a Municipal Flag to represent the city of Newport, and which committee consists of Mrs. Maud Howe Elliott, Rev. Roderick Terry, Miss Mary E. Harvey, Mr. John Nicholas Brown, Mr. Joseph G. Stevens, 2nd, Mr. John Howard Benson and Mr. A. O'D. Taylor, begs to report:

1st, That they have given time and thought to this matter and have aimed to secure the best advice on the subject from artists, designers and others.

2nd, Captain Byron McCandless, U.S.N., the national authority on flags was consulted by your committee and met with them on this subject. He later spoke publicly giving his views as to what a City Flag should be.

3rd, Your committee spread abroad the ideas gained, and offered two prizes, one of $100 and the other of $25, for the most suitable design that might be suggested by designers.

4th, The competition was open to all artists, designers or persons of Newport County.

5th, The prize money was secured through voluntary public subscription, the appeal being sanctioned by His Honor, Mayor Mortimer A. Sullivan.

6th, On Thursday, August 8, 1929 your committee met in the office of the board of canvassers and made their selections from the designs submitted.

7th, Owing to the absence from the city of Mr. Brown, Mr. Benson, and Ms. Harvey, their places on the committee were filled by Mr. William Cotton, Miss Louise Sturtevant and Miss Virginia Braman, who with Mrs. Elliott, Rev. Dr. Terry, Mr. Stevens, and Mr. Taylor formed the acting selective committee.

8th, the first prize was awarded to the design of the Old Stone Mill with a wreath of green leaves on a blue scroll with "Newport" in gold letters, on a white field, surrounded by gold fringe. It was submitted by Mr. John L. Smith.

9th. The second prize was awarded to the design submitted by Miss Marjorie Wilson and is also a flag with a white field, with shield in red and yellow quarterings on which are the emblems of the Old Stone Mill, the Liberty Tree, the Constellation and the Memorial Tower, a black scroll runs across the shield on which are the words "Liberty, Peace, Independence".

10th. The committee now has the honor and pleasure of handing over these suggested designs to your Honorable body, feeling that the object desired has been accomplished so far as it lies within their power.

11th. It is the expressed opinion of the Flag committee that it is quite possible that these designs may require some adjustments or alterations before one is accepted as "Newport's City Flag". Nevertheless they feel that the basis for a city flag is fairly laid before your Honorable body.

A. O'D. TAYLOR.

Chairman A. O'D. Taylor, after reading the flag committee's report, took occasion to thank those who co-operated. He requested that Mrs. Maud Howe Elliott present the prizes to the victors in the flag competition, and permission was granted.

Alderman Cozzens moved that the report and the designs be accepted and referred to the Representative Council, and it was so voted.

Alderman Mahan asked relative to suggested changes, and Mr. Taylor said they would be minor. Later, on Alderman Mahan's motion, a vote of thanks was extended the flag committee.

Mrs. Elliott said all the designs had shown much thought, and the two chosen seemed to be the best. We must remember that the flag, when chosen, will last for centuries, and great deliberation must be taken in the final choice.

Mrs. Elliott then presented a check for $100 to John L. Smith, who submitted the winning design, saying the name John Smith stands for much and congratulating him. She also presented a check of $25 to Miss Marjorie Wilson, who finished second.

9th, The second prize was awarded to the design submitted by Miss Marjorie Wilson and is also a flag with a white field, with shield in red and yellow quarterings on which are the emblems of the Old Stone Mill, the Liberty Tree, the Constellation and the Memorial Tower, a black scroll runs across the shield on which are the words "Liberty, Peace, Independence."

10th, The committee now has the honor and pleasure of handing over these suggested designs to your Honorable body, feeling that the object desired has been accomplished so far as it lies within their power.

11th, It is the expressed opinion of the Flag committee that it is quite possible that these designs may require some adjustments or alterations before one is accepted as "Newport's City Flag." Nevertheless, they feel that the basis for a city flag is fairly laid before your Honorable body.

A. O'D. Taylor.

Chairman A. O'D. Taylor, after reading the flag committee's report, took occasion to thank those who cooperated. He requested that Mrs. Maud Howe Elliott present the prizes to the victors in the flag competition, and permission was granted.

Alderman Cozzens moved that the report and the designs be accepted and referred to the Representative Council, and it was so voted.

Aldermen Mahan asked relative to suggested changes, and Mr. Taylor said they would be minor. Later, on Alderman Mahan's motion, a vote of thanks was extended to the flag committee.

Mrs. Elliott said all the designs had shown much thought and the two chosen seem to be the best. We must remember that the flag, when chosen, will last for centuries, and great deliberation must be taken in the final choice.

Mrs. Elliott then presented a check for $100 to John L. Smith, who submitted the winning design, saying the name John Smith stands for much and congratulating him. She also presented a check of $25 to Miss Marjorie Wilson, who finished second.

Recommendations made by the Librarian of the R.I. Historical Society

Howard Millar Chapin (1887-1940) was the Librarian of the Rhode Island Historical Society for 28 years. He wrote dozens of books on Rhode Island history, including the two-volume set, *A Documentary History of Rhode Island*.

He graduated from Brown University in 1908 and after a few years in the jewelry industry, he became the assistant business manager of the *Province Evening News*. In 1912, he married Hope C. Brown, the daughter of D. Russell Brown, who was the Governor of Rhode Island from 1892 to 1895.

A letter written on September 21, 1929, by Howard M Chapin,
Librarian of the
Rhode Island Historical Society
68 Waterman Street
Providence, R. I
Incorporated 1822

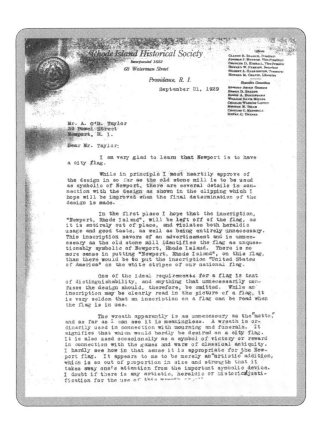

Mr. A. O'D. Taylor
39 Powell Street
Newport, R.I.

Dear Mr. Taylor:

I'm very glad to learn that Newport is to have a city flag.
While in principle I most heartily approve of the design in so far as the old stone mill is to be used as symbolic of Newport, there are several details in connection with the design as shown in the clipping which I hope will be improved when the final determination of the design is made.

In the first place I hope that the inscription, "Newport, Rhode Island," will be left off of the flag, as it is entirely out of place, and violates both heraldic usage and good taste, as well as being entirely unnecessary. This inscription savors of an advertisement and is unnecessary as the old stone mill identifies the flag as unquestionably symbolic of Newport, Rhode Island. There is no more sense in putting "Newport, Rhode Island", on this flag, than there would be to put the inscription "United States of America" on the white stripes of our national flag.

One of the ideal requirements of a flag is that of distinguishability, and anything that unnecessarily confuses the design should, therefore, be omitted. While an inscription may be clearly read in the picture of a flag, it is very seldom that an inscription on a flag can be read when the flag is in use.

The wreath apparently is as unnecessary as the motto, and as far as I can see it is meaningless. A wreath is ordinarily used in connection with mourning and funerals. It signifies that which would hardly be desired on a city flag. It is also used occasionally as a symbol of victory or reward in connection with the games and wars of classical antiquity. I hardly see how in that sense it is appropriate for the Newport flag. It appears to me to be merely an "artistic" addition, which is so out of proportion in size and strength that it takes away one's attention from the important symbolic device, I doubt if there is any artistic, heraldic or historical justification for the use of this wreath at all.

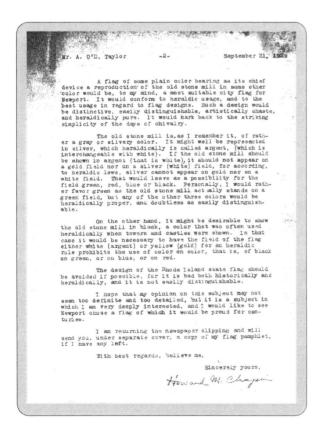

A flag of some plain color bearing as its chief device a reproduction of the old stone mill in some other color would be, to my mind, a most suitable city flag for Newport. It would conform to heraldic usage, and to the best usage in regard to flag designs. Such a design would be distinctive, easily distinguishable, artistically chaste, and heraldically pure.

It would hark back to the striking simplicity of the days of chivalry. The old stone mill is, as I remember it, of rather a gray or silvery color. It might well be represented in silver, which heraldically is called argent, (which is interchangeable with white).

If the old stone mill should be shown in argent (that is white) it should not appear on a gold field nor on a silver (white) field, for according, to heraldic laws, silver cannot appear on gold nor on a white field. That would leave as a possibility for the field green, red, blue or black. Personally, I would rather favor green as the old stone mill actually stands on a green field, but any of the other three colors would be heraldically proper, and doubtless as easily distinguishable.

On the other hand, it might be desirable to show the old stone mill in black, a color that was often used heraldically when towers and castles were shown. In that case it would be necessary to have the field of the flag either white (argent) or yellow (gold) for an heraldic rule prohibits the use of color on color, that is, of black on green, or on blue, or on red.

The design of the Rhode Island State flag should be avoided if possible, for it is bad both historically and heraldically, and it is not easily distinguishable.

I hope that my opinion on this subject may not seem too definite and too detailed, but it is a subject in which I am very deeply interested, and I would like to see Newport chose a flag of which it would be proud for centuries.

I am returning the newspaper clipping and will send you, under separate cover, a copy of my flag pamphlet, if I have any left.

With best regards, believe me,

Sincerely yours,

Howard M. Chapin

[Here are Howard M. Chapin's handwritten afterthoughts,
which were enclosed with the previous typewritten letter.
I have added the images of the flags for reference.]

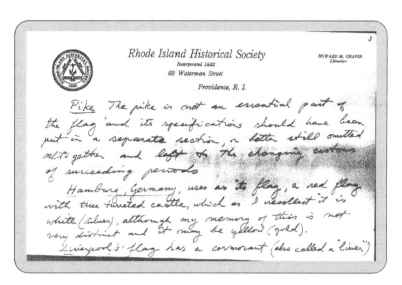

Flag of Hamburg, Germany

Flag of Liverpool, England

<u>Pike</u> [the flagpole] The pike is not an essential part of the flag and its specifications should have been put in a separate section, or better still omitted altogether and left to the changing customs of succeeding periods.

<u>Hamburg, Germany</u> uses as its flag, a red flag with three turreted castle, which as I recollect is white (silver), although my memory of this is not very distinct and it may be yellow (gold).

Liverpool's flag has a cormorant (also called a "liver") for its device. I do not remember the colors. The city is named for the bird called a liver.

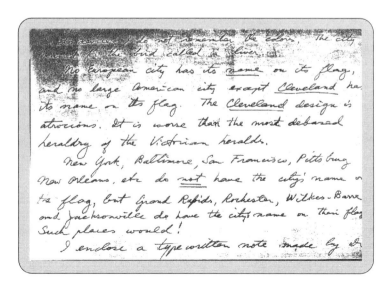

Flag of Cleveland

No European city has its name on its flag and no large American city except <u>Cleveland</u> has its name on its flag. The <u>Cleveland</u> design is atrocious. It is worse than the most debased heraldry of the Victorian heralds.

New York, Baltimore, San Francisco, Pittsburgh, New Orleans, etc. do <u>not</u> have the city's name on the flag, ...

Flag of New York

Flag of Baltimore

Flag of San Francisco

Flag of Pittsburg

Flag of New Orleans

Flag of Grand Rapids

Flag of Rochester

... but Grant Rapids, Rochester, Wilkes-Barre, and Jacksonville do have their city's name on their flags. Such places would!

Flag of Wilkes-Barre

Flag of Jacksonville

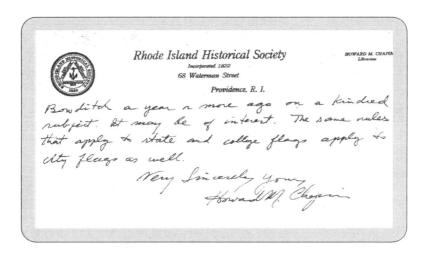

I enclose a typewritten note made by Dr. Bowditch a year or more ago on a kindred subject. The same rules that apply to state and college flag apply to city flags as well.

Very Sincerely Yours,
Howard M. Chapin

[Dr. Harold Bowditch, from Brookline, Massachusetts, was a well-known authority on heraldry. Bowditch's note, which Chapin refers to, has apparently been lost.]

A CHANGE IN THE WORDING ON THE FLAG

From John L. Smith's contest-winning design

The Newport City Flag Committee had a dilemma on their hands. RI's top authority on heraldry, Howard M. Chapin was pretty adamant that the word "Newport" NOT be put on the new City Flag.

But to have just a picture of the Old Stone Mill, surrounded by a wreath would seem rather plain. And they had already had held the contest, announced the winner, and presented their decision to the Aldermen. What where they to do?

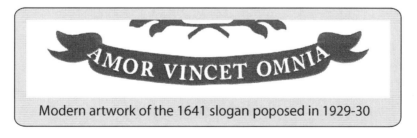

Modern artwork of the 1641 slogan poposed in 1929-30

Well, sometime between September 21, 1929, and April 4, 1930, someone came up with the idea of replacing the word "Newport" with the Latin phrase, *Amor Vincet Omnia*, commonly translated as "Love Conquers All."

This was not just some slogan someone selected out of the blue. It was used by the first English colonists on Aquidneck Island in 1641.

The proposed "Isle of Aquidneck" merger of 1641

The symbol for the 1641 proposed joint government between Newport and Portsmouth, to be called "Aqidneck" or the "Isle of Aquidneck"

Banished from Boston in 1638, Anne and William Hutchinson, William Coddington, William Dyer, John Coggeshall, Nicholas Easton, William Brenton, John Clarke, and others settled in Pocassett, later called Portsmouth, on the northern end of Aquidneck Island.

A year later, in 1639, Coddington, Dyer, Clarke, Brenton, Easton, and others moved to the beautiful harbor at the mouth of the Narragansett Bay to settle Newport.

Two years later, in 1641, the two towns decided to unify into one political entity called "Aquidneck" or the "Isle of Aquidneck."

Unfortunately, efforts to create this joint colony soon dissolved. It wasn't until 1647 that Newport and Portsmouth joined with Providence and Warwick to form a unified government.

However, on March 19, 1641, when Newport and Portsmouth were still in the process of merging to create the colony of "Aquidneck," item number 15 of their agreement stated:

> *15. It is ordered that a Manuall Seale shall be Provided for the State, & that the Signet or Engraveur thereof shall be a sheafe of Arrowes bound up and in the Liess or Bond this motto indented Amor vincett omnia.*

(Note that vincett is spelled with two t's.)

tnm at tne neaa or tne companie.
15. It is ordered that A Manuall Seale shall be Provided for the State, & that the Signett or Engraveur thereof shall be a sheafe of Arrowes bound up and in the Liess or Bond this motto indented Amor vincett omnia.
16. It is ordered that Ingagemt shall be taken by the

1641 "Aquidneck" union proposal, from Howard M. Chapin's 1916 *Documentary History of Rhode Island*

A "Manuall Seale," is a handheld metal seal that makes an imprint in hot wax. It is used to seal or authenticize documents. According to noted Rhode Island historian Sidney S. Rider, the word "Liess" is a corruption of the old English word "Lease," meaning a leathern thong (or leash) commonly used by falconers for their hawks and hounds.

It could have been Howard M. Chapin who came up with the idea of using, *Amor Vincet Omnia* for the flag, as he had reproduced the Aquidneck islander's 1641 agreement in his *Documentary History of Rhode Island*, published in 1916.

Chapin also reported about this 1641 colony of Aquidneck's "Manuall Seale" on page 48 of his 1930 book *Illustrations of the Seals, Arms, and Flags of Rhode Island.*

However, as we've seen, Chapin wasn't very enthusiastic about putting words on flags.

Newport Historical Society Seal, with the Society's rendition of the Aquidneck Seal of 1641

It might have been a member of the Newport City Flag Committee who suggested using the epithet, *Amor Vincet Omnia*. After all, it was engraved on the seal of the Newport Historical Society, which had been established back in 1854.

No images of the seal proposed in 1641 have ever been found (only the descriptive text). So the Newport Historical Society made their own interpretation: a crisscross array of 5 bound arrows and a banner above which reads *Amor Vincet Omnia*.

[Howard M. Chapin, *Illustrations of the Seals, Arms, and Flags of Rhode Island* (Providence, RI Historical Society, 1930)]

Recently, the Newport Historical Society has modernized its logo with color, shading, and a new typeface.

Modern day seal/ logo of the Newport Historical Society with a "sheaf of arrows" and "Amor Vincet Omnia"

So what does the "sheaf of arrows" signify?

Most likely the sheaf of arrows does not relate to the colonists' association with the Native Americans, who were quite skilled with bows and arrows.

To understand the symbolic meaning of "sheaf of arrows" in the Western tradition, we must travel back 575 BC.

Aesop, that fabulous fabulist, relates a story entitled: *A Bundle of Sticks*.

A father, whose sons were perpetually quarreling, decided to give them a practical illustration of the evils of disunion. He gave to each in succession a bundle of sticks and ordered them to break it. Though each son tried with all his strength, none succeeded.

The father then unbound the sticks and gave each son one of them, which they broke easily. Then he said: "My sons if you are of one mind, and unite to assist each other, you will be as this bundle, proof against your enemies. But if you are divided among yourselves, you will be broken as easily as these sticks.

[Michael Macrone, *It's Greek to Me!* (New York, Cader Books, 1991) p.26]

Aesop's fable: *A Bundle of Sticks*

In Roman Times, this metaphoric "bundle of sticks" was called a *fasces*.

Attendants of Roman magistrates would carry a *fasces*, a bundles of birch or elm rods bound by a red cord. Often an axe was included in the bundle and the exposed axe head would gleam in the sunlight. Strength in unity, or else.

Roman Magistrate's attendant carrying a "fascis" with axe enclosed

Coin with a "sheaf of arrows" minted during the reign of Queen Isabella I and King Ferdinand II of Spain

Queen Isabella I and Ferdinand II, who ruled Spain from 1474 to 1504, (and who sent Columbus off on his mission) used a "bundle of arrows" for their heraldic symbol.

Influential English Renaissance families, like the Leicesters and the Herberts, incorporated "a bundle of arrows" in their coats-of-arms.

(Written on the binding "leash" is the Greek word *Aplanos*, the Herbert family motto, which means "steadfast.")

A "sheaf of arrows" in the Herbert Family crest

Houdon's statue of George Washington in the rotunda of the Virginia Capitol building in Richmond

In 1768, just prior to the American Revolution, the patriot John Dickinson wrote, "By uniting we stand, by dividing we fall."

After the war, the American leaders adopted a bundle of 13 rods as a national symbol, each rod representing one of the 13 original colonies.

In the famous sculpture of George Washington by Jean-Antoine Houdon, which stands in the Virginia State Capitol Building, George's hand is resting on a fasces.

(There is an exact replica of Jean-Antoine Houdon's sculpture of George Washington overlooking the garden on the south side of the Redwood Library in Newport.)

The old Liberty Head dime has a fasces on its reverse side.

The fascis on the Liberty Head dime

One of the two fasces on the front wall of the U.S. House of Representatives

And still today, on the wall behind the Speaker's podium in the United States House of Representatives are two tall fasces.

Two bronze fasces on the front wall of the U.S. House of Representatives

The Eagle on the Great Seal of the United States is carrying 13 arrows in one of his talons.

13 arrows grasped by the talon of the eagle on the Great Seal of the U.S.

To summarize, when the citizens of Newport and Portsmouth proposed the use of a "sheaf of arrows" for their governmental seal, part of their intent was clearly "strength in unity."

But "arrows" are symbolic in other ways.

St. Sebastian with arrows

To devout Christians, which most all of these colonists were, the arrow was associated with someone who had dedicated his or her life to God. Exemplars of this tradition include Saint Sebastian, Saint Teresa, and Saint Ursula, who are each generally depicted with arrows.

Cupid shooting "arrows of love"

And as you know from Valentine's Day cards, the arrow has another potent meaning: **love**.

A Roman copy of "Cupid stringing his bow" originally created by the Greek sculptor Lisippos around 350 BC

The Greeks called their youthful god of love *Eros*, (which means "desire"). The Romans called their youthful god of love *Cupid* (which also means "desire"), but also by another name, *Amor* (which means "love").

Get shot by arrow from *Eros* or *Cupid/Amor*, and you are filled with uncontrollable desire.

"Amor Vincit Omnia" is the title of Caravaggio's painting of Cupid, completed in 1602

In 1602, the great Italian painter Caravaggio completed *Amor Vincit Omnia*, depicting Cupid wreaking havoc upon symbols of human endeavors, like musical instruments, geometry tools, and a pen with manuscript papers.

In Geoffrey Chaucer's "The Prioress's Tale," written around 1375 AD, the nun, Madame Eglantine, has a string of beads attached to a pendant that reads *Amor Vincit Omnia*.

To summarize, the Aquidneck colonists' 1641 "bundle of arrows" seems to have three meanings: "strength in unity," "devoted to God," and "Love."

The love symbolism of the arrows relates directly the subject of the motto, *Amor* or "Love."

VINCIT, VINCET, OR VINCETT?

The expression "Love Conquers All" was first popularized by the Roman poet Publius Vergilius Maro, commonly called Virgil, who lived from 70-19 BC.

Line 69 of his Tenth Eclogue (Eclogue means a "short poem") reads," ***Omnia vincit amor et nos cedamus amori,*** "Love conquers all so let us all yield to love,"

Virgil (70-19 BC) writes *"Omni Vincit Amor"* or *"Love Conquers All"* in line 69 of Eclogue X

Note that Virgil's sentence starts with ***Omnia***, not ***Amor***. In Latin the ordering of some of the words in a sentence is flexible, so these two phrases mean basically the same thing.

(Note that "all" in this context means "all things" not "all people." Had Virgil mean "love conquers all people" he would have said **Omnes** Vincit Amor.)

Also, Virgil spells the word "conquers" as ***vincit***, not ***vincet***, as it appears on the Newport City Flag.

Should it be spelled "Vincit" or Vincet"?

There is much debate as to whether the word
Vincet in *Amor Vincet Omnia* should be spelled
with an "*i*," as in *Vincit*, or with an "*e*" as in *Vincet*.

The difference is:
Vincit is the present tense: "Love Conquers All."
Vincet is the future tense: "Love Will Conquer All."

But there is actually a third option:
It's the way the colonists spelled it in their proposed "Isle of Aquidneck"
merger between Newport and Portsmouth in 1641: *Vincett* (with two *t*'s).

(Brian Melendez a Latin scholar from Minneapolis clarifies the particulars on the website called The Straight Dope:

"Vincere is a third-conjugation verb, so *vincit* is the third-person singular,
present tense, indicative mood, active voice, and thus translates as "conquers."

Vincet is the third-person singular, future tense, indicative mood,
active voice, and would translate as "will conquer.")

The "Vincit" argument

If you Google it, you'll find that *Amor Vincit Omnia*
is a much more commonly used expression.

Cicero (around 40 BC), Chaucer (around 1375),
and Caravaggio (in 1602) all spelled it *Vincit*.

"Love Conquers All" is a pithier expression than
"Love Will Conquer All." The 3-word version
sounds snappier than the 4-word version.

> ## AMOR VINCIT OMNIA
> ### LOVE CONQUERS ALL

Most people wouldn't want love to "conquer all" sometime in the future.
They'd want love to "conquer all" now, in the present.

The "Vincet" argument

The Flag Committee of 1929,
the persnickety expert Howard M. Chapin,
the Aldermen, and the Representative Council,
all approved the spelling *Vincet*.

All the previous versions of the
Newport City Flag have spelled it *Vincet*.

Since 1854, the Newport Historical Society's
logo has spelled it *Vincet* (that's 150 years).

That's a pretty long tradition.

> ## AMOR VINCET OMNIA
> ## LOVE WILL CONQUER ALL

In addition, the boy's name "Vincent"
(as in Van Gogh, Lombardi, or Diesel)
derives from the Latin name *Vincentius*.
And both are spelled with an "e."
(*Vincentius* means "conquering.")

The Vincett argument

> ## AMOR VINCETT OMNIA
> ## LOVE WILL CONQUER ALL

Vincett, with an extra "*t*," is how the colonists actually
spelled it in their own handwriting in 1641.

However, the colonists didn't have the strict spelling
rules we have today. They might have added the extra
letter to ensure the "*t*" was pronounced, and not silent.

[For example, if the colonists were to write, "Jimmy Buffet ate
lunch at the buffet," they might add an extra "t" to the end
of Buffet to indicate the difference in pronunciation (Buffett).]

The *Vincit* and *Vincet* enthusiasts might agree that
Vincett is the weakest of the three arguments.

It's the future tense (will conquer)
and it's not part of the Newport City Flag tradition.

A linguistic clue adds a new twist

To get an expert opinion, I asked Latinist Peter Barrios-Lech, Assistant
Professor of Classics at the University of Massachusetts in Boston.

Peter confirmed that ***Vincit*** is the present tense and ***Vincet*** is the future tense.

But he added there was "a certain ambiguity with "***Amor Vincit Omnia****.*"
It can mean 'Love **Binds** All' or it can mean 'Love **Conquers** All.'"

The Latin verb *vincio* means:
to bind, to fetter, to secure, or to restrain.

The Latin verb *vinco* means:
"to overcome, to defeat, to conquer, or to prevail."

Though yet their spelling is very similar, these two
verbs mean two completely different things.
(They are even abutting entries in all Latin dictionaries.)

To further emphasize this distinction, ***viniculum*** (the Latin
noun derived from ***vincio***) means a band (like the strap of the sandal),
or a cord (like the one used to tie up a ship) or fetters (prison chains).

On the other hand the verb from the verb ***vinco,*** we get the
English words, "invincible, convince, vanquish and victory."

In short, "Amor Vincent Omnia,"
might be read as "Love Conquers All,"
but it might also be read as "Love Restrains All."
(And the latter is not a very inspiring axiom.)

However, here's the twist:
Amor Vincet Omnia can **only** be read as "Love Will Conquer All,"
It can **never** be read as "Love Will Restrain All."

The two verbs, *vincio* (to bind) and
vinco (to conquer) are conjugated differently.

If, for some strange reason, one wanted to express "Love Will Bind All,"
it would be written ***Amor Vinciet Omnia***. (With both an "*i*" and an "*e.*")

How Virgil got away with using the ambiguous Amor Vincit Omnia

Virgil, around 35 BC, might have felt comfortable with the present tense, (*vincit*, or "conquers"), despite the possibility it might be mistaken for "binds," for a simple reason:

Omnia vincet amor is only the first half of Virgil's full line:
Omnia vincet amor et nos cedamus amori
or "Love conquers all, so let us yield to love."

The word *cedamus* is a form of the verb *cedo*,
meaning "to concede, yield, submit, or give in."
"Conceding" is the flip side of "conquering."

In other words, the verb in the second half of
the sentence clarifies the verb in the first half.

Virgil
70-19 BC

Were the early colonists aware that borrowing only three words
from Virgil's full line would lead to a possible misinterpretation?
And, to prevent that from happening, they took the
safe route by using *vincet* (shall conquer) instead?

Perhaps the scholars on the 1929 Flag Committee know about this situation as well.
(Though I have found no written discussion about it.)

All this is a very strong argument in favor of the "Vincet" alternative,
aside from the fact that it's such a well-established tradition.

Chaucer used Amor Vincit Omnia BECAUSE of its ambiguity

Most scholars agree that Chaucer's portrayal of the nun
he calls the "Prioress" is a satire on the hypocrisy of the Medieval
church at the time. Her words, actions and adornments reveal her
inner yearning to be an aristocrat rather than a woman of the cloth.

To use Chaucer's term she is a "counterfete." As Paul
Beekman Taylor writes in *Chaucer Translator*:

Chaucer
1343-1400

> "Counterfeiting as translation is common in Chau-
> cer's works. Among the frequent Latin examples of it
> is the inscription Amor vincit omnia on the Prioress
> gold brooch, which renders both "love conquers all"
> and "love ties all in a knot" (from *vinco* and *vincio*
> respectively.). The latter reading, overlooked by
> many readers, is pertinent to the brooch's function as
> a connection for two strings of beads, or prayers."

The idea that *Amor Vincit Omnia* could be taken in two ways was probably the very reason Chaucer decided to use it. This intentional irony would have been understood by wise readers in the Middle Ages, in the Renaissance (Shakespeare "borrowed" story lines from Chaucer), by learned English colonists in the 1600's, and perhaps by the scholars on the 1929 Flag Commission.

[Paul Beekman Taylor, *Chaucer Translator*, (Lanham, MD, University Press of America, Rowman and Littlefield, 1998)]

The talented painter Caravaggio was not a well-versed wordsmith, but he was a pompous pimp.

Michelangelo Merisi da Caravaggio (1571-1610) was a ground-breaking painter, but he was not a writer. He was an orphan at the age of 11 and in his teens was the apprentice to a painter in Milan. In his 20's, he moved to Rome and became popular for his "tenebrism," a technique that used dark shadow to make the light areas really shine.

Personality-wise, Carravagio had an arrogant streak. He was always getting into arguments and picking fights.

Biographer Andrew Graham-Dixon claims Caravaggio was a pimp who stole a prostitute from his rival, the notorious Roman pimp, Ranuccio Tomassoni. In the resulting duel, Caravagio killed Tomassoni with a swift sword to the groin.

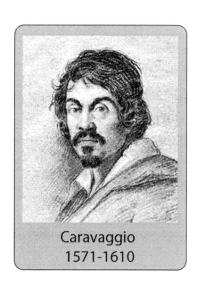

Caravaggio
1571-1610

To avoid jail time, Caravaggio fled Rome to the Isle of Malta, where he joined the Knights of Malta military order. Not really cut out for the discipline of the military, he ended up in jail for assaulting Fra Giovanni Rodomonte Roero, one of the Order's most senior knights. After a daring escape from his underground prison cell, Caravaggio fled to Naples. But a year later, Roero tracked him down at a tavern and slashed his face and eyes. Caravaggio died within a year, at age 38.

The point of this brief, yet graphic, biography is that Caravaggio was not a scholar of literature. He wasn't even close to being in the same league as Virgil and Chaucer. Caravaggio probably "borrowed" the first three words of Virgil's line in the Eclogue (and even his best friends wouldn't want to inform him it might be misinterpreted).

[Andrew Graham-Dixon, *Caravaggio, A Life Sacred and Profane* (New York and London, Penguin Books, 2010)]

Summary of Virgil, Chaucer and Caravaggio

So Virgil's *Amor Vincit Omnia,* is misleading because
it has been plucked out of its defining context.

Chaucer's *Amor Vincet Omnia* is
intentionally a tongue-in-cheek satire.

And Carravagio's Amor Vincet Omnia comes
from a hot-headed painter, borrowing just
the pithy part of Chaucer expression,
apparently ignoring the ambiguity.

Shall we consider a different translation?

Some scholars don't see much difference between *vincit* and *vincet.*

They say the present tense implies something happening
not just now, but ongoing (like "Love *Always* Conquers All").

And the future tense draws a conclusion about that
which is ongoing (like "Love *Will Always* Conquer All").

Furthermore, I have a suggestion that will address any criticism that
"Amor Vincet Omnia", or "Love Will Conquer All," only implies future-time.

Instead of translating it as "Love **Will** Conquer All," how about translating
it as "Love **Shall** Conquer All." The words "Will" and Shall" are synonyms.
But there are some shades of difference between them.

Amor Vincet Omnia

Love Shall Conquer All

When first considering the translation "Love Shall Conquer All," it sounded sort of old-fashioned to my American ear. It sounded pseudo Shakespearean. It sounded a little haughty or pretentious. We Americans wouldn't say "Shall we go get a cheeseburger?"

However in England, the use of the word "Shall" is perfectly normal. Say the following sentence with a British accent and you'll see it sounds fine: "Shall we have a spot of tea?" The English aren't trying to sound pretentious, it's just how they speak.

With this in mind, let's step back in time. The early colonists of Rhode Island weren't American, they were British. America wasn't founded until 136 years later, after the Revolutionary War. And even then, 90% of Americans were descendants of English colonists.

Nowadays, our modern American English language is an amalgamation of influences from Spanish, Irish, Italian, West African, Native American and many other languages.

How can I be so sure the colonists of 1641 would have used the word "shall"?

Because the word "shall" is in primary documents, written in their own handwriting!

At the General Court of August 6, 1640, Portsmouth and Newport agreed "that each town **shall** have the transaction of the affairs that **shall** fall within their own town."

It was also to be each town's responsibility to keep a "Towne Book" to record land sales, "which **shall** be a clear evidence for them and theirs, to whom it is so granted."

They didn't mean the "transaction records" and creating the two "Towne Books" was something to be done in the future. They meant "effective immediately."

[my bold; Rhode Island *Colonial Records*, I, p. 106 and 114; cited in, Dennis Allen O'Toole, *Exiles, Refugees, and Rogues: The Quest for Order in the Towns and Colony of Province Plantations 1636-1654*, (Newport, Cosmopolite Press, 2014), pp. 174-5]

On March 1, 1653, when there was still disharmony
between the towns on Narragansett Bay, a friend of
the colony from England, Cornelius Holland, wrote
a letter admonishing the local leaders to lay aside:

"all prejudices that may be crept in amongst you,
… soe **Shall** you Finde peace among yourselves &
Further Favor (noe doupt) in the eyes of the Councell
[the authorities back in London], Soe **shall** you strengthen
the hands of those in whose heart is to doe you good…"

(my bold; Rhode Island *Colonial Records,* I, p. 240; O'Toole, page 425)

Cornelius Holland's letter highlights another
interesting characteristic of the word "shall":
It's lofty.

The word "shall" is used by orators in uplifting prose.
It implies strong determination. It emphasizes certainty.

Most of the 10 Commandments include "shall:
"Thou shalt not steal."

(and the Commandments were probably intended to be take effect immediately.)

In his famous Gettysburg address, Lincoln resolves,
"that these dead **shall** not have died in vain… That this
nation, under God, **shall** have a new birth of freedom."

Martin Luther King exhorts "We **shall** overcome."

In short, *Amor **Vincet** Omnia,* "Love Shall Conquer All,"
cannot be mistaken for "Love Shall Bind All."

It speaks to the future as well as to the present.
And it has an air of determination and importance.

But then again, Virgil, Caravaggio, and Chaucer are really the roots of Amor **Vincit**
Omnia. And the three word translation "Love Conquers All" certainly is catchy.

And *Vincett* is what the colonists actually wrote.

What do you think?
Vincit, Vincet, or *Vincett*?
(More ideas about this debate later.)

There Was a Lot Going On in 1929

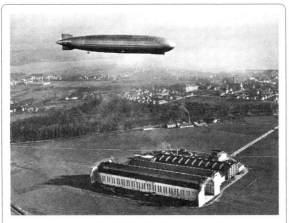

In August of 1929, the German airship, Graf Zeppelin, circumnavigated the globe

In August 1929, the Graf Zeppelin circumnavigated of the globe.

Starting in Lakehurst, New Jersey, she flew across the Atlantic to Germany. This photo shows her at the refueling station in Friedrichshafen, Germany, her home port, where she had been built.

The Graf Zeppelin then crossed over northern Siberia to Tokyo for another refueling. Then across the Pacific to Los Angeles. Then back to Lakehurst, New Jersey. All in 21 days and 5 hours.

On **Black Tuesday**, October, 29, 1929, the stock market crashed, sending the U.S. and world economy into a tailspin.

On the bright side, Aquidneck Island was about to be connected with northern Rhode Island: Bristol, Warren, Barrington, and Providence.

(Prior to the construction of the Mount Hope Bridge Newporters had to use the Stone Bridge that connected Portsmouth with Tiverton and then go to Fall River in order to get to Providence. Or they could take the ferry to Jamestown, cross the island, and then take another ferry to the South County.)

PAGE TEN   NEWPORT HERALD, THURSDAY, OCTOBER 24, 1929

The Span That Unites The State--Mount Hope Bridge

Dream of years now an actuality, a massive $4,000,000 structure of steel and concrete—To be Dedicated and opened with fitting ceremonies at noon today.

RHODE ISLAND'S FIRST HIGH ROAD OF THE SKIES READY FOR PUBLIC USE

TODAY- SURELY "HERBIE'S" DAY

H. W. Smith Sees Successful Termination Of Bridge Battle

CLOUDY AND -COLDER SAYS WEATHER MA

Exciting Times

A zeppelin flew around the globe for the first time. The Stock Market crashed. The Mount Hope Bridge opened. And something *really* big was about to occur in Newport, in September of 1930.

In these exciting times, the Newport City Flag Committee evidently felt it appropriate to reintroduce "Love Conquers All" as a motto for Newport.

This motto had felt right in the past, it felt right then, and they knew this timeless expression would feel right in the future.

ALDERMEN APPROVE CITY FLAG DESIGN

After the gloomy winter following the October crash, spring of 1930 finally arrived. The Board of Aldermen convened and sent a "Recommendation of Adoption" for the Newport City Flag to the Representative Council.

Newport Herald
Friday, April 4, 1930

ALDERMEN APPROVE CITY FLAG DESIGN
Sent to Council with Recommendation of Adoption.

The design of the city flag, the winner of the competition held a year or so ago by the flag commission appointed to conduct the contest, was given the board of aldermen's stamp of approval last night at the weekly meeting of the board. It was sent along to the representative council recommended for adoption, but the suggestion is to be made to the commission to have the date of the founding of the city 1639 inserted on the flag under the Old Stone Mill or central design.

The matter came before the alderman through a communication from the flag commission A. O'D. Taylor, chairman with which was submitted a framed design of the flag and a request for early action on the part of the official bodies of the city.

The mayor said it was a pretty design. He would like to see the date 1639 on it also, something to distinguish it as Newport's flag. As much time has been given to the flag it was voted for the board to give its approval to the design and that the matter be referred to the Council recommended.

On motion of Alderman Mahan it was recommended that the flag commission consider placing the date on the flag. On motion of Alderman Cozzens, the design will be hung in the lower hall of the City Hall.

[Apparently, the Mayor's idea of including the date 1639 on the flag was rejected. Not only would it add another confusing design element, it would make it appear as though the Old Stone Mill was built in 1639.]

THE REPRESENTATIVE COUNCIL APPROVES THE NEWPORT CITY FLAG

CITY OF NEWPORT

REPRESENTATIVE COUNCIL

RESOLVED: That the design of the City Flag of the
City of Newport as submitted to the Representative Council
by the Commission on City Flag be adopted and approved.
The design shall bear a drawing of the Old Stone Mill, enclosed within an irregular circle of leaves and underneath
the Old Stone Mill and the leaves there shall be a blue
banner and on the banner there shall be inscribed the words
AMOR VINCET OMNIA.

          For the purpose of identifying the design
or drawing submitted by the Commission on City Flag the Mayor
and City Clerk of the City of Newport shall sign the design
and the design shall thereupon be deposited in the office
of the City Clerk of the City of Newport and shall be and
continue to remain a part of the records of that office.

In Representative Council,
          August 26, 1930.

The Newport Representative Council officially
adopted the Newport City Flag on August 26, 1930

On the reverse side of the
document is handwritten:

*Resolution:
adopting the
design of the City
flag of the City
of Newport*

---

*August 26, 1930
Passage Recommend
Com. [Commission] on Resolutions etc.
W.P. Sheffield
Chairman.*

*In Representative Council
August 26, 1930
Read and passed
W. Norman Sayer
City Clerk*

**Signatures on the reverse side
of the Representative
Council's Resolution**

WHAT SPECIAL EVENT WAS ABOUT TO TAKE PLACE IN NEWPORT IN SEPTEMBER OF 1930?

This is a story about a young boy born in Glasgow, Scotland in 1850, named Tommy Lipton.

His parents, Thomas and Frances Lipton, sold ham, eggs, and butter in a small mom-and-pop grocery store.

Despite their limited income,
they made sure their son,
Tommy Jr., attended
St. Andrew's Parish School.

Tommy left school at age thirteen
to help support his parents.
He worked as a printer's
errand-boy, a shirt-cutter,
and a cabin boy.

At the age of 15, he saved up for a
ticket to the land of opportunity:
America.

Arriving with eight dollars in his pocket, he spent five years
in various states, working as a tobacco planter in Virginia,
a door-to-door salesman in New Orleans,
and a grocer's assistant in New York City.

Returning to Glasgow, he expanded his
parents business into "Lipton's Market."
Soon he had a chain of six stores in Scotland.

By 1888, when he was 38, he had 300 stores all across England.

In 1890, he visited Ceylon, the island of Sri Lanka.

He bought five huge plantations and started importing his own tea.

This allowed Lipton to sell tea at half the price other merchants needed to charge.

If there was something Thomas Lipton loved more than tea and making money, it was sailing.

With his competitive spirit, he wanted to be the best— he wanted to win the America's Cup!

A brief history of the America's Cup.

In 1851, Great Britain's Royal Yacht Squadron challenged the New York Yacht Club to race around the Isle of Wight, off the southern coast of England.

The New York Yacht Club's schooner *America* won the race. Not only did the next event move to the United States, but the cup was renamed after the yacht *America*.

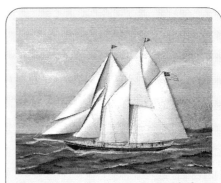

The "America's Cup" was named after the victorious schooner *America*

England was eager to see the cup return, but in their next eight attempts, from 1872 to 1895, the New York Yacht Club won every America's Cup Challenge.

At the turn of the century, Sir Thomas Lipton was determined to bring the cup home to England. But it was not to be.

In 1899, Lipton's **Shamrock I** lost in three straight races. In 1901, Lipton's **Shamrock II** lost in three straight races. In 1903, Lipton's **Shamrock III** lost in three straight races.

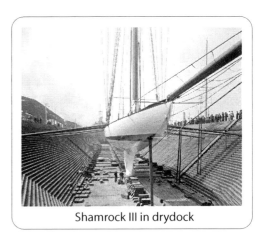

Shamrock III in drydock

The dapper Sir Thomas Lipton

The King of England, Edward VI, shared Lipton's passion for yachting, and he knighted the self-made millionaire: "Sir Thomas Lipton."

Because World War I, the races were cancelled for many years.

Then in 1920, Sir Thomas Lipton challenged again with *Shamrock IV*. Again, he lost in three straight races.

In 1930, Sir Thomas Lipton turned 80 years old.

He put all he could into the design of *Shamrock V*.
It had a steel frame, a mahogany deck, and a
hollow spruce mast as tall as a 16-story building.

A new rule had been instituted.
It was no longer the best of 5 races,
it was the best of 7.

The America's Cup

Americans love the World Series and the Super Bowl.
But in England, baseball and American football aren't very popular sports.

However, the island nation is proud of its centuries-long sailing tradition.
And the challenge for the America's Cup was not your average regatta.
It was the rebellious child versus the Mother country:
an echo of the Revolutionary War.

Sir Thomas Lipton had even made it to the front
cover of *Time* magazine, during an earlier
challenge, back in November 3, 1924.

Harold Stirling Vanderbilt

But, Sir Thomas Lipton was competing against one of the most formidable skippers in America's Cup history: the railroad magnate, Harold Stirling Vanderbilt.

On September 15, 1930 Harold Vanderbilt made it to the front cover of *Time* magazine.

Vanderbilt captained the *Enterprise*, with its hidden, lightweight winches and the first durable aluminum mast.

Over 300 news reporters and photographers from around the world flocked to Newport for the races.

Part of the fleet of pleasure craft which followed the racing *Enterprise* and *Shamrock V* Saturday. Hundreds of boats, ranging from small motor craft to big steam yachts, followed the progress of the race.

Thousands of people watched the races from "pleasure boats" and from the rocky shore at Brenton Point.

In the first race, *Enterprise* beat *Shamrock V* by three minutes.

In the second race, *Enterprise* won by ten minutes.

In the third race, *Shamrock V* took the early lead. But, in a tacking duel, a halyard broke, and the mainsail came crashing down on the deck.

67

Alas, Shamrock also lost the fourth.

Sir Thomas Lipton was heard to utter despondently,"I can't win."
He returned to England, only to die the following year.

Thomas Edison and Sir Thomas Lipton

But after five attempts, over a period of
31 years, Sir Thomas Lipton had endeared
himself to the American public.

They admired Sir Thomas Lipton
for being a self-made man.
Rags to riches.

NOT THE "CUP", BUT A TROPHY NEVERTHELESS

Sir Thomas Lipton with the replica of the Old Stone Mill, presented him by the city of Newport.

By Daily News Photographer

For the 1930 challenge, a citizen's committee, led by Rhode Island State Senator William H. Vanderbilt, had arranged for a dinner to honor Sir Thomas Lipton.

The committee also commissioned the design of a 12-inch-tall sterling silver replica of the Old Stone Mill.

They had considered giving Lipton a "gold-mounted cane," but it was finally decided that the Old Stone Mill "was more distinctive of Newport."

The 300 newspaper correspondents and the crews of the two sloops received silver pencils.

was largely attended.
There was some discussion regarding the recommendation of the souvenir committee, which had the replica of the Old Stone Mill, specially designed and standing 12 inches high, as the first choice, and a gold-mounted cane as the next. It was finally decided that the Old Stone Mill was more distinctive of Newport, despite the fact that there

SIR THOMAS, LIPTON, HOLDING THE NEWPORT CITIZENS' GIFT

LEFT TO RIGHT—MAYOR MORTIMER A. SULLIVAN, EDWARD A. SHERMAN, SENATOR WILLIAM H. VANDERBILT, LEANDER K. CARR, WILLIA M GOODMAN.
By Daily News Photographer

This photograph from the September 26, 1930 *Newport Mercury* newspaper shows Sir Thomas Lipton holding the Old Stone Mill replica.

To the left of Sir Thomas Lipton is Sen. William H. Vanderbilt, and on the far left is Newport Mayor Mortimer A. Sullivan, who was Mayor of Newport for 12 years, from 1923 to 1935.

Before he died, Sir Thomas Lipton bequeathed the Old Stone Mill replica to Glasgow Museum, where it still can be seen today.

The one-foot-tall sterling silver replica of the "Old Stone Mill," given to Sir Thomas Lipton in 1930, is currently in the Glasgow Museum.

THE NEWPORT CITY FLAG FLEW FOR THE FIRST TIME DURING THE FIRST RACE!

On Monday, September 15, 1930, the *Newport Daily News* published a picture of Mayor Mortimer A. Sullivan delivering the "City Flag" to Mr. and Mrs. Aymar Johnson on their yacht Enchantress, "where it flew for the first time," during the first race, on Saturday, September 13, 1930.

CHARLES F. HOFFMAN, JR.

Mrs. Aymar Johnson, was the former Miss Marion K. Hoffman, daughter of Charles Frederick Hoffman, a wealthy New York City real estate broker and developer.

In 1903, Charles Frederick Hoffman purchased Armsea Hall, a neoclassical Palladian villa designed by Beaux-Arts architect Francis Laurens Vinton Hoppin.

Its large portico, with four tall Corinthian columns, overlooked the East Passage of Narragansett Bay, which connects Newport Harbor to the sea.

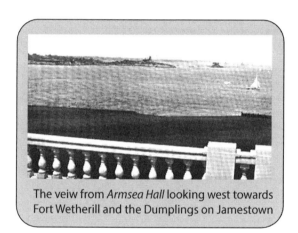

The veiw from *Armsea Hall* looking west towards Fort Wetherill and the Dumplings on Jamestown

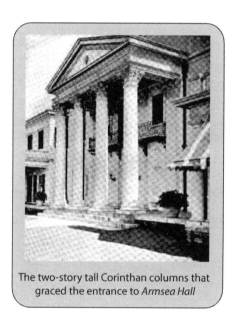

The two-story tall Corinthan columns that graced the entrance to *Armsea Hall*

Its rooms were spacious ...

... and it featured one of the finest rose gardens in Newport.

The property abutted the Auchincloss family's Hammersmith Farm, the childhood summer home of Jacqueline Bouvier Kennedy.

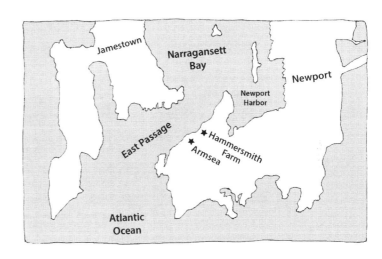

Interestingly, Jack and Jackie had privately leased Armsea Hall from Marion and Aymar Johnson for the months of August and September of 1964.

Unfortunately, it never became the summer White House, as Kennedy was tragically assassinated in November of 1963.

I've been unable to find any photographs of the vessel *Enchantress*. But if it was anything like *Armsea Hall*, it was obviously no dinghy.

The official Newport City Flag first flew on
September 13, 1930, above the yacht
Enchantress, which was following the
first race of the America's Cup Challenge

THE "OLD STONE MILL" AS A SYMBOL OF NEWPORT

In the early 1900s, people came from all over America to see the mysterious stone tower—an architectural connection to the Old World.

They weren't sure who built it, but they knew there was nothing else like it in America.

Its image graced dinner plates, ...

... cups and mugs, ...

... serving trays, ...

... spoons and pendants, ...

... and numerous postcards.

The citizens knew the solidly-constructed "Old Stone Mill" had stood in the heart of Newport since the 1600's and they knew it would stand for centuries to come.

An enduring symbol of the City (surrounded) by the Sea.

Bird's eye view of Newport in 1878

The origin of the name "Hotel Viking"

Most of the mansions on Bellevue Avenue were built during Newport's Gilded Age, which lasted from around 1850 to the beginning of the 1900s. After World War I, wealthy Americans were lured to the warm-all-year resorts in Florida and Southern California.

In 1924, to help attract visitors to Newport, several businessmen teamed up to build a grand hotel at the northernmost end of Bellevue Avenue. To find a suitable name, they held a city-wide naming contest. Out of 722 entries, they chose the name "Hotel Viking." Historians at that time thought the Old Stone Mill, just around the corner in Touro Park, was built by the Vikings around 1150 A.D.

Just as the 1929 Flag Committee had determined, the hoteliers agreed the Old Stone Mill best symbolized Newport. Today you can still see a clock in the lobby with runic numbers or you can get married in the huge Skoal Room. (Skoal is Old Norse for "Cheers!")

Incidentally, one of the team of Hotel Viking entrepreneurs was William P. Sheffield. You might recognize that name. He was the city Representative Councilman who signed the Resolution adopting John L. Smith's flag design, which has the "Viking" tower on it.

THE NEWPORT CITY FLAG FROM 1930 TO 1970

Apparently, during the depression of the 1930 and the war years in the 1940's, the use of the Newport City flag slowly faded.

The 1950's: an inquiry about the Newport City Flag

In the Wednesday, June 10, 1953 *Newport Daily News*, E.E.E., the writer of a column called "**The Grist Mill**" inquired:

Has the City of Newport an official flag? If so, what does it look like, and what motto, if any, does it carry? These are questions asked by a Grist Mill reader. We recall that one of Newport's mayors some years ago used to fly the Newport flag from his office window on all occasions when the flag should be displayed.

There were actually three editors at the Daily News who contributed to The Grist Mill column. Their names each had an initial "E." Thus the joint byline, E.E.E. The column was later written, single-handedly, for almost 30 years, by Leonard J. Panaggio.)

Two days later, on Friday, June 12, 1953, E. E. E. reports in the The Grist Mill that John L. Smith, himself, wrote in to recount his story of winning the 1920 Newport City Flag contest:

Newport has an official flag according to John L. Smith of Mill Lane, Portsmouth. He should know because he designed it back in 1929. Mr. Smith, a former Newport resident and a mason by trade, has dabbled in art.

The flag has a fringe of gold with a field of white, in the center of which is a green laurel wreath enclosing a replica of the Old Stone Mill. A blue ribbon below contains the name Newport in gold. This later was changed to an inscription "Amor Vincet Omnia," meaning "Love Conquers All Things."

This flag, sometimes called the mayor's flag, was flown for the first time from the masthead of yacht Enchantress, owned by Mr. and Mrs. Aymar Johnson of Armsea Hall on September 13, 1930, during an America's Cup yacht race here. Aboard the yacht at the time was Mayor Mortimer A. Sullivan. Prior to the race, the flag flew from the Ida Lewis Yacht Club flagpole.

Later the flag was given to Sir Thomas Lipton who was competing for the cup with Shamrock IV, [Shamrock V] the last of his four [five] unsuccessful attempts to win the cup. At the time, Lipton said he would take it back to Ireland [Scotland] to place in his trophy case.

Three days later, on Monday, June 15, 1953, "E. E. E." reports about his (or her) investigations at the City Hall flag locker:

(The locker no longer exists today.)

If anyone is looking for a city flag, in the City Hall flag locker there are two large flags, three small flags and a handkerchief-sized flag.

When the fire department had its huge national flag from the USS Wyoming, with 46 stars, it used to be hung on holidays and auspicious occasions from the City Hall balcony. It would be flying with the two city flags, one from the aldermanic chamber windows and the other from the School Department windows.

The large flag has gradually given in to the wear of time and has not been used lately. However, Newporters memory must be short or no one bothered to look at flag decorations not to recall the city's flag.

This in 1953 publicity still failed to stir much interest in reviving the use of the Newport City Flag.

Six years later. in 1959...

Six years later, on February 27, 1959, E. E. E. quizzes the public about the flag:

When was the City of Newport flag adopted and who was its creator? The question arose when the flag was shown in a photograph taken about 30 years ago. The Old Stone Mill, surrounded by a wreath, under which was the motto: "Amor Vincet Omnia" (Love Conquers All) are on a field of white.

THE GRIST MILL

E. E. E.

An answer to a Grist inquiry and a fine suggestion on a Newport city flag were received from Mrs. Edward M. Karoli of Bristol. She said that in August, 1929, a committee headed by the late Alexander O'D. Taylor conducted a contest for a design of a city flag. The entry of her father, John L. Smith, formerly of Almy Street, was the winner. Smith, now retired, and his wife travel considerably, are now in Florida, and usually take an apartment in Warren summers, she said. Mrs. Karoli suggested that the city make small souvenir city flags to be passed out to tourists and others, as done in other areas. Cars visiting Newport, if adorned with such flags, could carry them many places to advertise Newport, she believes.

• • • •

were exhibited last fall at the Art Association. In fact, the students' drawings are still stored there and may be seen by anyone who is interested, President William H. Drury tells us.

The schemes were on the grandiose side, but it sometimes takes an outsider, with no predigested notions, to show a boldness in design and perspective that is needed. Those on the scene are often too close to the trees to see the forest as a whole. Incidentally, Charles Bourgeois of Boston, whose Jazz Festival position of field coordinator puts him close to the practical side of things, was at Princeton for the final consultation and evaluation of the student architects' plans. 'Tis something of a feather in the community cap for

About a month later, on April 6, 1959,
E. E. E. got a response from Mrs. Edward M. Karoli:

An answer to a Grist inquiry and a fine suggestion on a Newport city flag were received from Mrs. Edward M. Karoli of Bristol. She said that in August, 1929, a committee headed by the late Alexander O'D. Taylor conducted a contest for a design of a city flag. The entry of her father, John. L. Smith, formerly of Almy Street was the winner. Smith, now retired, and his wife travel considerably, and are now in Florida, and usually take an apartment in Warren summers, she said.

Mrs. Karoli suggested that the city make small souvenir city flags to be passed out to tourists and others, as done in other areas. Cars visiting Newport, if adorned with such flags, could carry them many places to advertise Newport, she believes.

A FLAG FIT FOR A QUEEN
DURING
AMERICA'S BICENTENNIAL YEAR,
1976

Leo Waring was a patriotic Newporter. And not just because he was born on the Fourth of July. Or because he died on May 4, the day Rhode Island declared independence from England (back in 1775).

Leo was so patriotic, in 1975, he urged Newport Mayor Humphrey Donnelly and Senator Claiborne Pell to ask President Gerald R. Ford President to make Newport a stop on the Presidential Bicentennial Tour in the following year, 1976.

The trio flew to Washington, and on July 17, 1975. They met with President Ford in the White House. The *Daily Diary of President Gerald R. Ford* reports:

The purpose of the meeting was to receive a replica of the 'Newport Artillery Company Flag' produced by the Ebenezer Flag Company.

(Earlier that morning, President Ford had met with Henry Kissinger, Donald Rumsfeld, Dick Cheney and the Chief of the CIA).

Scanned from the President's Daily Diary Collection (Box 76) at the Gerald R. Ford Presidential Library

THE WHITE HOUSE

THE DAILY DIARY OF PRESIDENT GERALD R. FORD

PLACE DAY BEGAN	DATE (Mo., Day, Yr.)
THE WHITE HOUSE	JULY 17, 1975
WASHINGTON, D.C.	

TIME DAY
7:40 p.m. THURSDAY

TIME		PHONE	ACTIVITY
In	Out		
7:40			The President went to the Oval Office.
7:42	8:00		The President met with: David A. Peterson, Chief, Central Intelligence Agency/Office of Current Intelligence (CIA/OCI) White House Support Staff Lt. Gen. Brent Scowcroft, Deputy Assistant for National Security Affairs
8:05			The President went to the State Dining Room.
8:05	9:50		The President hosted a breakfast meeting to discuss restoration of U.S. military assistance to Turkey with Members of Congress. For a list of attendees, see APPENDIX "A."
9:50			The President returned to the Oval Office.
9:55	10:32		The President met with: Henry A. Kissinger, Secretary of State
10:00	10:32		Lt. Gen. Scowcroft
10:36	11:05		The President met with: Donald H. Rumsfeld, Assistant
10:58	11:05		Robert T. Hartmann, Counsellor
10:58	11:05		Max L. Friedersdorf, Assistant for Legislative Affairs
10:58	11:05		Richard B. Cheney, Deputy Assistant
10:58	11:05		Ronald H. Nessen, Press Secretary
			CONGRESSIONAL HOUR
11:05	11:08		The President met with: Senator Ted Stevens (R-Alaska) Congressman Don E. Young (R-Alaska) Patrick E. O'Donnell, Deputy Assistant for Legislative Affairs The purpose of the meeting was to receive a relief map of the state of Alaska which has been sculpted from remnants of the steel and piping used in the Alaska pipeline.
11:10	11:16		The President met with: Senator Claiborne Pell (D-Rhode Island) Humphrey Donnelly, Mayor (D-Newport, Rhode Island) Leo Waring, President of Ebenezer Flag Company, Newport, Rhode Island Mr. O'Donnell The purpose of the meeting was to receive a replica of the "Newport Artillery Company Flag" produced by the Ebenezer Flag Company.
11:16			The President went to the Rose Garden.
11:16	11:23		The President met with: Congressman Elford A. Cederberg (R-Michigan) Congressman Marvin L. Esch (R-Michigan) Vernon C. Loen, Deputy Assistant for Legislative

The following year, the President had a surprise for Leo Waring. The President and First Lady would be accompanied by the Queen of England.

And Leo Waring had a surprise for the President. At his own expense, Leo made a giant U.S. flag, 30 feet tall by 50 feet wide. He also made two smaller U.S. flags, each 20 feet tall by 30 feet wide.

AMERICA'S 200TH YEAR was marked July 4 by Newport Artillery Company firing off 21-gun salute on Washington Square. American flag on former Navy YMCA is 30 by 50 feet, and is reputedly largest ever made in state. Aquidneck Island volunteers helped make flag for Ebenezer Flagg Co.

This photo caption reads:

AMERICA'S 200th YEAR *was marked July 4 by Newport Artillery Company firing off 21-gun salute on Washington Square. American flag on former Navy YMCA is 30 feet by 50 feet, and is reputedly largest ever made in state. Aquidneck Island volunteers help make flag for Ebenezer Flagg Co.*

[Leo Waring cleverly named his flag company after Sergeant Ebenezer Flagg, a soldier in the Revolutionary War.]

Newport awaits visit
of Britain's monarch

By T. CURTIS FORBES

Here, where the Colonists 200 years ago declared their independence from the Crown two months before the rest of the colonies. Queen Elizabeth II will conclude the formal aspect of her tour of those "colonies" with a state dinner with President Ford.

The Queen is scheduled to fly here this afternoon after a busy morning in Connecticut, the Constitution State, and a mid-day celebration at the University of Virginia.

On his way to dinner with the Queen, President Ford will stop in Plattsburgh, N.Y. to give a send-off speech to members of the U.S. Olympic team leaving for Montreal.

Once here, the two heads of state will maintain vastly different profiles, the President's being virtually totally private and the Queen's as public as British Royalty ever gets.

Local police, security officers from both countries, a variety of state agencies and the U.S. Coast Guard have set up elaborate precautions unrivalled in the history of the state.

The most public part of the Queen's visit will be dedication ceremonies of Queen Anne Square at 3:55 p.m. She may also be seen during her motorcade from the Newport Bridge along Washington Street to Long Wharf, where Rochambeau marched to meet General Washington.

The entourage will turn right on America's Cup Avenue and will pass by the HMS Rose, replica of the British frigate that blockaded this harbor during the Revolution.

Driving up Memorial Boulevard, the Royal party will pass St. Mary's Church, oldest Catholic parish in the state and where the late President John F. Kennedy married the former Jacqueline Bouvier.

The motorcade will then proceed down Spring Street for the ceremony, which will take place just about the same time that the President's party will be arriving at the Naval Education and Training Center (NETC).

That group will fly here from the Otis Air Force Base. Members of the President's group will include Vice President Nelson Rockefeller, Secretary of State Henry Kissinger, Secretary of Commerce Eliot Richardson their wives and other members of the administration.

The base will be opened only to persons normally allowed there and the Coast Guard will provide strict security in the vicinity of the Queen's yacht the Britannia.

The ship is expected at Destroyer Pier One about 4:45 p.m. If the weather is as good as predicted, the yacht might cruise in the lower half of Narragansett Bay during the dinner.

Police have added extra men for the historic visits but declined this morning to predict the size of the crowds at the base and along the line of motorcade.

Weather conditions appear to be ideal for the evening's activities. Skies are supposed to be perfectly clear this evening with a zero chance of precipitation. Temperatures will be in the mid '60s and winds will be light and variable on the bay.

Making the night even more attractive will be a moon only one day short of being full.

After the historic dinner, the President is slated to return to Washington. The Royal yacht will head for Boston for Bicentennial festivities there tomorrow.

QUEEN ELIZABETH II waves to crowd from balcony of Lincoln Center's New York State Theater yesterday. British monarch will be in Newport today for dedication of Queen Anne Square, and later will be host to President Ford for dinner aboard royal yacht Britannia. (UPI)

Newport Daily News
Saturday, July 10, 176

Newport awaits visit of Britain's monarch
By T. Curtis Forbes

Here, where the Colonists 200 years ago declared their independence from the Crown two months before the rest of the colonies, Queen Elizabeth II will conclude the formal aspect of her tour of those "colonies" with a state dinner with President Ford.

The Queen is scheduled to fly here this morning after a busy morning in Connecticut, the Constitution State, and a mid-day celebration at the University of Virginia.

On his way to dinner with the Queen President Ford will stop in Plattsburgh N.Y. to give a send-off speech to members of the U.S. Olympic team leaving for Montreal.

Once here, the two heads of state will maintain vastly different profiles, the President's being virtually totally private and the Queen's as public as British Royalty ever gets.

Local police, security officers from both countries, a variety of state agencies and U.S. Coast Guard have set up elaborate precautions unrivaled in the history of the state.

The most public part of the Queen's visit will be the dedication ceremonies of Queen Anne Square at 5:55 p.m. She may also be seen during her motorcade from the Newport Bridge along Washington Street to Long Wharf, where Rochambeau marched to meet Gen. Washington.

The entourage will turn right on America's Cup Avenue and will pass by the HMS Rose, a replica of the British frigate that blockaded this harbor during the Revolution.

Driving up Memorial Boulevard, the Royal party will pass St. Mary's Church, oldest Catholic parish in the state and where the late President John F. Kennedy married the former Jacqueline Bouvier.

The motorcade will then proceed down Spring Street for the ceremony, which will take place just about the same time that the President's party will be arriving at the Naval Education and Training Center (NETC).

That group will fly here from the Otis Air Force Base. Members of the President's group will include Vice President Nelson Rockefeller, Secretary of State Henry Kissinger, Secretary of Commerce Elliott Richardson, their wives and other members of the administration.

The base will be opened only to persons normally allowed there and the Coast Guard will provide strict security in the vicinity of Queen's yacht, the Britannia.

The ship is expected at Destroyer Pier One about 4:45 p.m. If the weather is as good as predicted, the yacht might cruise in the lower half of Narragansett Bay during the dinner.

Police have added extra men for the historic visits but declined this morning to predict the size of the crowds at the base and along the line of the motorcade.

Weather conditions appear to be ideal for the evening's activities. Skies are supposed to be perfectly clear this evening with a zero chance of precipitation. Temperatures will be in the mid-60s and winds will be light and variable on the bay.

Making the night even more attractive will be a moon only one day short of being full.

After the historic dinner, the President is slated to return to Washington. The Royal yacht will head for Boston for Bicentennial festivities there tomorrow.

The photo caption reads:

Queen Elizabeth II *waves to crowd from balcony of Lincoln Center's New York State Theater yesterday. British monarch will be in Newport today for dedication of Queen Anne Square, and later will be host to President Ford for dinner aboard Royal yacht Britannia. (UPI)*

Large crowd eagerly waits for Queen at Trinity Church

People started gathering on Spring Street across from Trinity Church Saturday afternoon some three hours before Queen Elizabeth was expected. Placed behind a rope on the east side of the street, the group grew to several hundred before being allowed into a public viewing area on the church grounds at 4:30.

But before they were let into the church grounds, the people good naturedly jostled each other back and forth across the restraining rope. A man in shorts, evidently with some authority, kept striding back and forth across the front of the crowd, admonishing everyone to stay behind the barrier. Shortly before 4:30, the police called a tow truck to haul away a car parked across the street from the church.

Secret Service men checked women's handbags but gave the men only a cursory glance as they admitted them into the viewing area, the rear of which also was roped off. Local officials and others who called and asked for passes were admitted to the front part of the viewing area.

Among those who showed up in the more restricted front area were John J. Egan, who has been conducting a rear guard action against the Newport Redevelopment Agency over his property and sign that blocked the view of Trinity Church from the foot of what is to be Queen Anne Square.

The vertical smokestack bearing the sign was taken down on agency orders Saturday after vandals evidently weakened the cables holding it up. Agency officials said the removal of the smokestack and sign had nothing to do with the Queen's appearance here.

The Queen finally arrived at 6:35, some 40 minutes after she was scheduled to get here. She passed through the ranks of the Artillery Company of Newport. The crowd behind the second rope broke through to join the others in the front reserved area.

Newport Daily News
Monday, July 12. 1976

Large crowd eagerly waits
for Queen at Trinity Church

People started gathering on Spring Street across from Trinity Church Saturday afternoon, some three hours before Queen Elizabeth was expected. Placed behind a rope on the side of the street, the group grew to several hundred before being allowed into a public viewing area on the church grounds at 4:30.

"But before they were led into the church grounds, the people good-naturedly jostled each other back and forth across the restraining rope. A man in shorts, evidently with some authority, was striding back and forth across the front of the crowd, admonishing everyone to stay behind the barrier. Shortly before 4:30, the police called a tow truck to haul away a car parked across the street from the church.

Secret Service men checked women's handbags, but gave the men only a cursory glance as they admitted them into the viewing area, the rear of which also was roped off. Local officials and others who called and asked for passes were admitted to the front part of the viewing area.

Among those who showed up in the more restricted front area was John J. Egan, who had been conducting a rear guard action against the Newport Redevelopment Authority over his property and sign that block the view of Trinity Church from the foot of what is to be Queen Anne Square.

The vertical smokestack bearing the sign was taken down on agency orders Saturday after vandals evidently weakened the cables holding it up. Agency official said the removal of the smokestack and sign had nothing to do with the Queen's appearance here.

The Queen finally arrived at 6:35, some 40 minutes after she was scheduled to get here. She passed through the ranks of the Artillery Company of Newport. The crowd behind the second rope broke through to join the others in the front reserved area.

On July 10, 1976,
President Ford,
First Lady Betty Ford,
Queen Elizabeth II
and her husband,
Prince Philip,
arrived in Newport.

In a ceremony just outside of Trinity Church dedicating Queen
Anne Square, Leo Waring had a surprise for the Queen:
a brand new version of the old Newport City Flag.

A HIGH POINT OF AMERICA'S Bicentennial Year was dedication of Queen Anne Square outside historic Trinity Church by Britain's Queen Elizabeth II, shown receiving Newport flag from Mayor Donnelly. Legend says, 'Love Conquers All.' Elizabeth's consort, Prince Philip, Duke of Edinburgh, stands between Queen and mayor. July 10 event drew huge crowds to lawn of church.

This picture appeared in the *Newport Mercury* on Friday, December 31,1976, as part of the year-end wrap-up. The photo caption reads:

A HIGH POINT OF AMERICA'S *Bicentennial Year was the dedication of Queen Anne Square outside historic Trinity Church by Britain's Queen Elizabeth II, shown receiving the Newport flag from Mayor Donnelly. Legend says, "Love Conquers All." Elizabeth's consort, Prince Philip, Duke of Edinburgh, stands between the Queen and the Mayor. The July 10 event drew huge crowds to lawn of church.*

(To design this new edition of the flag, Leo Waring probably referred to the September 15, 1930 photo of Mayor Mortimer A. Sullivan giving the flag to Mr. and Mrs. Aymar Johnson aboard their yacht *Enchantress*.)

When this same photo originally appeared in the *Newport Mercury*
on July, 11, 1976, the photo caption read:

RECEIVING OLD *Newport flag from Mayor Donnelly is Queen Elizabeth II, during dedication ceremony of Queen Anne Square Saturday. Queen's husband, Prince Philip, Duke of Edinburgh, watches presentation. Flag designed many years ago by Newport resident, was reproduced by Ebenezer Flagg Co. from photograph. (Daily News)*

About a month after the Queen's visit on July 12, some thieves had a surprise for Leo Waring. They stole the 20-by-30 foot flag that had been flying above Long Wharf Mall!

Thieves nab big U.S. flag

Monday, July 12

A large American flag which provided visitors to the city with one of its most colorful sights has been stolen from its place on top of a flagpole on Long Wharf. The 20 by 30 foot flag, valued at $350 by the Ebezener Flagg Co., which lent it to the city, was stolen between 2:30 and 7:30 a.m. Sunday.

Davis Leys, president of the Downtown Business Council, said today the Council had posted a $100 reward for its return or the arrest of the thieves. Newport policemen have begun collecting a fund to be added to this reward, Capt. Norman Anderson said today.

College has ceremony for retiree

Louis O. Humes of 231 Miantonomi Ave. Middletown, was recently retired with more than 34 years of government service in an ceremony held at the Naval War College.

Leys said he was "extremely upset" over the incident and described the high-flying flag as the real "focal point of the area."

A spokesman for the Ebezener Flagg Co. said the flag was on indefinite loan to the city, because the company wished to offer it as a good will gesture to the city of Newport, and because it was an "impressive sight for visitors from the Tall Ships and those here to seen the Queen." He said the flag was one of two purchased from the Valley Forge Flag Co. in Pennsylvania.

The Fire Department volunteered to lower the flag at sunset and raise it at sunrise. This was done for some time until illumination of the flag was begun at night. It was then decided to display it day and night, because of its impressive beauty when illuminated, firemen said.

Patrolman Edward Schuster saw the flag flying at 2:30 a.m. Sunday when he was on patrol. At 7:30 a.m. Deputy Chief John Oakley looked out of the window at fire headquarters and ob-

Newport Mercury

Thieves nab big U. S. Flag

Monday, July 12

A large American flag, which provided visitors to the city with one of its most colorful sights, has been stolen from its place on top of a flagpole on Long Wharf. The 20 by 30 foot flag, valued at $350 by the Ebenezer Flagg Co., which lent it to the city, was stolen between 2:30 and 7:30 a.m. Sunday.

David Leys, president of the Downtown Business Council, said today the Council had posted a $100 reward for its return or the arrest of the thieves. Newport Policemen have begun collecting a fund to be added to this reward, Capt. Norman Anderson said today.

Leys said he was "extremely upset" over the incident and described the high-flying flag as the real "focal point of the area."

A spokesman for the Ebenezer Flagg Company said the flag was on indefinite loan to the city, because the company wished to offer it as a good will gesture to the city of Newport, and because it was an "impressive site for visitors from the Tall Ships and those here to see the Queen." He said the flag was one of two purchased from the Valley Forge Flag Co. in Pennsylvania.

The Fire Department volunteered to lower the flag at sunset and raise it at sunrise. This was done for some time until illumination of the flag was begun at night. It was then decided to display it day and night, because of its impressive beauty when illuminated, firemen said.

Patrolmen Edward Schuster saw the flag flying at 2:30 a.m. Sunday when he was on patrol. At 7:30 a.m. Deputy Chief John Oakley looked out the window of fire headquarters at fire headquarters and observed the flag was missing.

But only nine days later, on July 21, the police had a surprise for Leo Waring. They had found the flag.

Police recover huge flag stolen from Long Wharf

Wednesday, July 21

Old Glory has been recovered.

The 20-by-30-foot American flag, stolen July 11 from its place atop a flagpole on Long Wharf Mall, was recovered yesterday by Newport police.

Detectives said today "a number of leads" were followed, and after investigation the Stars and Stripes was found. Police said the flag is at the station, and David P. Leys, president of the Downtown Business Council, has been notified.

The Council had offered a $100 reward for information leading to recovery of the flag and the arrest of the thieves. Police would not say if arrests have been made.

Will Old Glory fly again at the mall?

"I hope so," said Leys, "but we'll have to come up with better security measures to prevent another theft. The Business Council may take it up with the city."

Leys credited Newport police for its efforts in tracking down the missing flag, which was an impressive sight for visitors here for the Tall Ships late last month, and for Queen Elizabeth II July 10.

The huge flag had been on indefinite loan to the city from the Ebenezer Flagg Co., because the company wished to offer it as a good will gesture to the City-by-the-Sea.

Patrolman Edward Schuster last saw the flag flying at 2:30 a.m. July 11 while he was on patrol. About five hours later, Deputy Chief John Oakley looked out the window at fire department headquarters on West Marlborough Street and noticed the banner was missing.

Newport Mercury

Police recover huge flag stolen from Long Wharf

Wednesday, July 21

Old Glory has been recovered.

The 20-by-30-foot American flag, stolen July 11 from its place atop a flagpole on Long Wharf Mall, was recovered yesterday by Newport police.

Detectives said today "a number of leads" were followed and after investigation, the Stars and Stripes was found. Police said the flag is at the station, and David P. Leys, president of the Downtown Business Council, has been notified.

The Council had offered a $100 reward for information leading to recovery of the flag and the arrest of the thieves. Police would not say if arrests have been made.

Will Old Glory fly again at the mall?

"I hope so," says Leys, "but we'll have to come up with a better security with measures to prevent another theft. The Business Council may take it up with the city."

Leys credited Newport police for its efforts in tracking down the missing flag, which was an impressive sight for visitors here for the Tall Ships late last month, and for Queen Elizabeth II July 10.

The huge flag had been on indefinite loan from the city from the Ebenezer Flagg Co, because the company wished to offer it as a good will gesture to the City-by-the-Sea.

Patrolmen Edward Schuster last saw the flag flying at 2:30 a.m. July 11 while he was on patrol. About five hours later, Chief deputy Chief John Oakley looked out the window at fire department headquarters on West Marlborough Street and noticed the banner was missing.

April 26, 1980

Newport flag Islander's idea

By JOAN K. BENNETT
Daily News Wire Editor

Although Newport is a city steeped in history, few residents are aware of how the City-by-the Sea got its flag.

It all began about 51 years ago, Aug. 15, 1929, to be exact. On that date, stone mason John L. Smith of 24 Almy St. won a Newport-wide competition to design a city flag. A commission, headed by the late A. O'D. Taylor, selected Smith's design and gave him $100. The prize was considered a substantial amount even in those days.

Smith is the husband of the late Pauline Johnson Smith, a native Newporter. As a mason, he followed his father's trade. But except for the artistic talent he used around the house, he was not a trained artist.

"Father chose the things he though Newport stood for in designing the flag," said Pauline Smith Karoli, his daughter. She said the Old Stone Mill is the focus of the flag, because it is representative of the city's rich history. The original design also had a gold fringe, a green laurel wreath of peace and a blue ribbon banner with the word "Newport" in gold on it.

By contrast, the city flag of today bears the words "Amor Vincet Omnia" (Love Conquers All Things) and no fringe. The changes were made soon after the 1929 contest at the suggestion of flag experts.

The Newport flag was flown for the first time on the yacht Enchantress, owned by Mr. and Mrs. Aymar Johnson of Armsea Hall on Sept. 15, 1930. Its use indicated Mayor Mortimer A. Sullivan was aboard the yacht for the local race scheduled that day. The mayor presented the flag to the Johnsons. Later, it was flown at the Ida Lewis Yahct Club.

During the 1930s, the flag's fame spread. An individual known as Commodore Lipton announced during one of the area "J" sailboat races that he was taking a Newport flag back to Europe to fly in his flagroom.

As for the father of the Newport flag, he and his wife moved to the Terraces in Portsmouth, when he retired as a mason. They operated a restaurant for a while and then moved to Florida, a favorite vacation spot of theirs.

At 86, Smith remains a very active individual in Ocala, Fla. Mrs. Smith died about 14 years ago. Besides their daughter, they have two sons, Robert A. Smith of Clearwater, Fla., and the late John W. Smith, who died in World War II.

Newport Daily News
April 26, 1980

Newport flag Islander's idea

by JOAN K. BENNETT
Daily News Wire Editor

Although Newport is a city steeped in history, few residents are aware of how the City-by-the Sea got its flag.

It all began about 51 years ago, August 15th, 1929, to be exact. On that date, stone mason John L. Smith of 24 Almy St. won a Newport-wide competition to design a city flag. A commission headed by the late A. O'D. Taylor selected Smith's design and gave him $100. The prize was considered a substantial amount even in those days.

Smith is the husband of the late Pauline Johnson Smith, a native Newporter. As a mason, he followed his father's trade. But except for the artistic talent he used around the house, he was not a trained artist.

"Father chose the things he thought Newport stood for in designing the flag," said Pauline Smith Karoli, his daughter. She said the Old Stone Mill is the focus of the flag, because it is representative of the city's rich history. The original design also had a gold fringe, a green laurel wreath of peace and a blue ribbon banner with the word "Newport" in gold on it.

90

By contrast, the city flag of today bears the words "Amor Vincet Omnia" (Love Conquers All Things) and no fringe. The changes were made soon after the 1929 contest at the suggestion of flag experts.

The Newport flag was flown for the first time on the yacht Enchantress, owned by Mr. and Mrs. Aymar Johnson of Armsea Hall on September 15, 1930. Its use indicated Mayor Mortimer A. Sullivan was aboard the yacht for the local race schedule that day. The mayor presented the flag to the Johnsons. Later, it was flown at the Ida Lewis Yacht Club.

During the 1930s, the flag's fame spread. An individual known as Commodore Lipton announced during one of the area "J" sailboat races that he was taking a Newport flag back to Europe to fly in his flagroom.

As for the father of the Newport flag, he and his wife moved to the Terraces in Portsmouth, where he retired as a mason. They operated a restaurant for a while and then moved to Florida, a favorite vacation spot of theirs.

At 86, Smith remains a very active individual in Ocala, Florida. Mrs. Smith died about 14 years ago. Besides their daughter they have two sons, Robert A. Smith of Clearwater, Fla. and the late John W. Smith, who died in World War II.

1984
A NEWPORT-TO-NEWPORT
FLAG PRESENTATION

FLAG SWAP — Mayor Patrick G. Kirby, left, gives Newport city flag to Brian G. Sullivan, at right, whose Newport Cultural Exchange Program plans to trade flag with city of Newport on Isle of Wight, England. Also at presentation ceremony Tuesday morning in City Hall is state Sen. Robert J. McKenna, center.

Ron Manville/Daily News

In 1984, a spark of interest in the city flag was kindled by G. Brian Sullivan, affectionately known as "Doctor Love." As the director of the Newport Cultural Exchange Program, he arranged to exchange flags with the British city of Newport.

As the capital of the Isle of Wight, on the south coast of England, Newport was the site of the first race of what later became known as the America's Cup challenge.

The caption of this photo in the
Wednesday, March 21, 1984,
Newport Daily News reads:

Flag Swap—Mayor Patrick G. Kirby, left, gives Newport city flag to G. Brian Sullivan, at right, whose Newport Cultural Exchange Program plans to trade flags with city of Newport on the Isle of Wight, England. Also at the presentation ceremony Tuesday morning in City Hall is State Senator Robert J. McKenna, center.

(Note that the Mayor has another Newport City Flag in his office, on a stand on the back right-hand side.)

The Grist Mill
(by Leonard J. Panaggio)

A READER IN ORLANDO, FLA., Mrs. Robert E. Hamann has written to ask a few questions about Newport,

"I wonder," she writes, "if you could check on an item for me. My brother-in-law, Konrad Damm, who owned Konrad's Shoe Store on Thames Street, and I share in getting The Newport Mercury every week and have for years. The Grist Mill is the first thing I look for. I have noticed several times that you have checked on items for people.

"On May 1 you had a picture of a young man presenting a city flag his company designed. This is what I would like to you to check for me. Many years ago, John L. Smith of Newport designed a city flag and, I believe, it also had the Old Stone Mill in a wreath of the center. He entered a contest and his flag was accepted. I'm not quite sure the details, but I know his flag was accepted.

"Many old Newport will remember the beautiful painting he did on the old Morton Park Garage. It was a huge painting of an Indian on horseback advertising Mohawk tires. Ray Armstrong owned the garage at that time. John Smith was quite an artist!

"One more thing, please. Whatever happened to the project of making a small shopping center out of the Paramount Theater? I saw a picture of that and remember the gold grill on each side of the theater.

"I also understand that dear, old Hazard's Beach is no more. My old stomping ground, what a shame!"

"I love Newport and your paper."

On May 10, a footnote to a letter to the editor in the Daily News told of the Newport flag competition. This was not published in the Mercury, so for the benefit of Mrs. Hamann and other Mercury readers, the Grist Mill reprints it:

The Newport flag competition was held in 1929 under the direction of the special committee of which the late A. O'D. Taylor was chairman. The winner of the prize offered was John L. Smith, a stonemason who lived on Almy Street. Street. His design, however, was somewhat altered later at the suggestion of flag experts. His flag had the Old Stone Mill enclosed in a laurel wreath and the words "Newport, R. I." in gold underneath. The flag had a gold fringe. The fringe and the city's name in gold were taken off and replaced by a blue ribbon on which is the motto Amor Vincet Omnia (Love Shall Conquer All).

The original project to remodel the Paramount ran into financial problems. A new owner recently announced that he will carry the shopping center idea to completion.

Hazard's Beach is still as active as ever."

When John L. Smith died in 1985 (at age 91)
he had two great-great-grandchildren

John L. Smith

CRYSTAL RIVER, Fla. — John L. Smith, 91, formerly of Portsmouth, R.I., designer of the Newport, R.I. city flag, died Saturday at the Spanish Gardens Nursing Home, Dunedin. He was the husband of the late H. Pauline Johnson Smith.

Born in Fall River, Mass., Oct. 27, 1893, he was a son of the late James and Elizabeth Leishman Smith. He served as an Army sergeant during World War I.

Mr. Smith, a stone mason all his life, worked with his father for members of Newport's summer colony until joining the federal civil service at the Navy Public Works Department in Newport. He retired in 1947 and came to Florida in 1961.

He was a member of the Conover Leary Post, American Legion; a member of the Newport Artillery Company since 1909; and a member of the Seamen's Church Institute of Newport.

Mr. Smith leaves a daughter, Pauline Karoli of Bristol, R.I.; a son, Robert A. Smith of Clearwater; a sister, Mrs. Thomas Byrley of Plainfield, N.J.; five grandchildren, six great-grandchildren and two great-great-grandchildren. He was the father of the late John W. Smith, who died while serving with the Army Air Corps during World War II.

Private committal services were conducted this morning in St. Mary's Churchyard, Portsmouth, by the Rev. Gordon Stenning, rector of St. Mary's Episcopal Church.

(Obituary for)
John L. Smith
(October 1893 – September 1985)

CRYSTAL RIVER, Fla. — John L. Smith, 91, formerly of Portsmouth R. I., designer of the Newport, R. I. City flag, died Saturday at the Spanish Gardens Nursing Home, Dunedin. He was the husband of the late H. [Hannah] Pauline Johnson Smith.

Born in Fall River, Mass., October 27, 1893, he was the son of the late James and Elizabeth Leishman Smith. He served as an Army sergeant during World War I.

Mr. Smith, a stone mason all his life, worked with his father for members of Newport's summer colony until joining the federal civic service at the Navy Public Works Department in Newport. He retired in 1947 and came to Florida in 1961.

He was a member of the Conover Leary Post, American Legion; a member of the Newport Artillery Company since 1909 [at age 16]; and a member of the Seamen's Church Institute of Newport.

Mr. Smith leaves a daughter, Pauline Karoli of Bristol, R.I.; a son, Robert A. Smith of Clearwater; a sister, Mrs. Thomas Byrley of Plainfield, N. J.; five grandchildren, six great-grandchildren and two great-great-grandchildren. He was the father of the late John W. Smith who died while serving in the Army Air Corps during World War II.

Private committal services were conducted this morning in St. Mary's Churchyard, Portsmouth, by the Rev. Gordon Stenning, rector of St. Mary's Episcopal Church.

Restoring
John L. Smith's design
of the original
Newport City Flag

Newspaper photos and articles provided helpful clues, but my goal was to locate an original Newport City Flag.

Fortunately, the Representative Council's 1930 Resolution stated that John L. Smith's drawing "was deposited in the office of the City Clerk, and shall be and continue to remain a part of the records of that office."

Unfortunately, the drawing has been lost. The current City Clerk, Kathleen Sylvia, and the Deputy City Clerk, Laura Swistak, searched diligently, but the oversize drawing was not filed in the same box as the 1930 Resolution. And several years ago there had been a flood in the Record Room. Many documents had to be thrown out. A dead-end.

A second possibility arose when one of "The Grist Mill" articles mentioned that Sir Thomas Lipton had been given a Newport City Flag as a token of appreciation in 1930.

Unfortunately, none of the three museums and Glasgow, Scotland that house the Lipton Archives had any record of that Newport City Flag.

I inquired at the various historical societies and libraries in Newport, the Newport Artillery Company, with Bert Duguay the retired owner of the Ebenezer Flagg Company, and local antique dealers. Nobody had an original Newport City Flag.

Then I found another clue. The Grist Mill article from April 6, 1959 mentioned that John L. Smith had a daughter, Mrs. Edward Karoli of Bristol. Googling around, I found Mr. and Mrs. Edward Karoli had a daughter named Jean Karoli. Further, I found this daughter was married and was now Jean Cioe of Crystal River, Florida.

When I phoned her, Jean was delighted that someone was interested in her grandfather, John L. Smith. But what she said next really surprised me. She still had the artwork that her grandfather had submitted for the 1929 flag contest!

Original artwork! Wow!
That was even better than finding an old flag!

Jean's son, Joseph, (who had fond memories of his great-grandfather) photographed the artwork and e-mailed it to me.

John L. Smith's 1929 prize-winning design for the Newport City Flag
(before the word Newport was replaced)
The gold border on three sides represents gold fringe.

The illustration, which had been rolled as a scroll all these years, was indeed John L. Smith's original contest winning design. Thus, it had the word "NEWPORT" on the blue banner. I knew the "revised" version that was once in the City Hall records room would have had "AMOR VINCET OMNIA" on it.

By studying the typeface John L. Smith used for the word NEWPORT, at least I knew what the letters N, E, O, R, and T looked like. And the W, (with its long middle point) provided a clue about what an M might look like. And it was not hard to create the letters I and A in a similar style. Thus I had all the letters of AMOR VINCET OMNIA.

The illustration of the Old Stone Mill was slightly faded and stained. But with a little digital optimization, I was able to bring back the original tone and contrast. I could tell John L Smith was a talented artist. He, fairly accurately, drew the approximately 1000 rocks that can be seen in this view of the Old Stone Mill. He used subtle shading to give the architecture a sense of roundness.

Surprisingly, even the leaves on the wreath were painted with various shades of green (from dark evergreen to spring green). Each leaf had a different shape and gesture, while the two stems arched in a perfect circle.

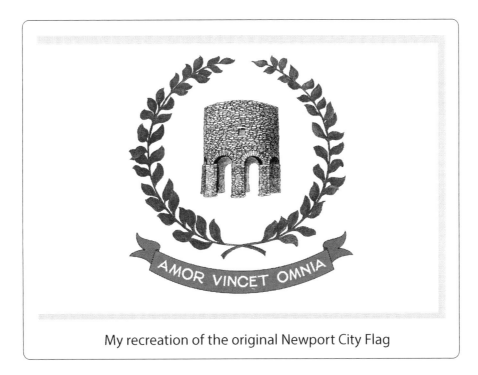

My recreation of the original Newport City Flag

Even though I was re-creating the Newport City Flag using John L. Smith's winning artwork, I had to acknowledge that John might have changed a few things in his finished AMOR VINCET OMNIA version, which had been submitted to the Representative Council.

Traces of evidence that a larger banner was once glued over John L. Smith's original artwork

On the original artwork there are hints that a larger banner was once glued over the smaller "Newport" banner. (Blue over-smudges and glue spots). But if the finished version was to remain in City Hall, this might have only been a working prototype. Unfortunately, we might never know what the finished version looked like.

It occurred to me that there was a bright side to the fact that the finished version got lost in time. It meant that there was no truly definitive version. Thus, it's up for interpretation.

The Newport City Flag which flew above the yacht Enchantress on Saturday, September 13, 1930

Looking closely at the Old Stone Mill in the first Newport City Flag, which flew on September 15, 1930, I estimated it had about 600 stones, a lot fewer than John L. Smith's 1000.

Back then, the flag was probably hand painted on canvas. Using a paintbrush instead of a sharp pen, it would be challenging to make the drawing too detailed.

Yet this is an important historical version of the flag. After all, this version was given as a token of appreciation to Sir Thomas Lipton, the man who spent millions trying to recapture the America's Cup for his friend, Edward VI, King of England,

Leo Waring's 1976 version of the Newport City Flag

Leo Waring's 1976 version only has about 50 stones, and has radiating lines in the arches, representing the spaces between the stones.

But this is also an important version of the flag. After all, Queen Elizabeth II of England still has this version, somewhere in one of her Royal Palaces.

All these aforementioned depictions are clearly recognizable as the Old Stone Mill. Indeed there are numerous other creative ways to visually interpret the Old Stone Mill.

Peter Tyler's multi-colored rendition of the Newport City Flag

For example, artist Peter Tyler has created colorful bumper stickers featuring the flag using bright orange, hot pink and purple.

Sometimes songs "covered" by different artists can actually be better than the original song. While we are appreciating history, we should also be making history. Times change. People change. Cultures change.

Perhaps it's OK to let the city flag change with the ages.

For example, in 1929, the idea of printing flags in full color (4-color) had not yet been invented.

Perhaps a full-color picture of the Old Stone Mill, an actual photograph of a laurel wreath, and a modern typeface would be an acceptable interpretation.

Maybe some day they will make a 3-D holographic version of the flag.

That "Vincet," "Vincit," or "Vincett" debate

As for the spelling of the Latin Word verb "to conquer,"
I think "VINCIT" (conquers),
and VINCET (shall conquer),
and "VINCETT" (shall conquer)
are **all** valid.

In fact, I think a version with the English words
"Love Shall Conquer All" would be appropriate.

Or even the short-and-sweet, present-tense version,
"Love Conquers All."

Or as some like to translate it,
"Love Conquers All Things."

We should think of the flag as a concept, not as an object. As long as it embodies the ideas of "success, history, and love," it's a Newport City Flag.

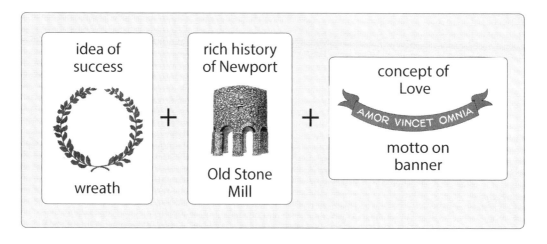

| idea of success | rich history of Newport | concept of Love |
| wreath | Old Stone Mill | motto on banner |

Here's a good example of "changing times." The flag itself has a touch of historical irony in it. The early Puritans in New England didn't celebrate Christmas. They felt wreaths and holidays were corrupting, pagan influences.

Yet the flag has the Aquidneck Islander's specially chosen motto, with a wreath above it. The colonists would not be amused, but nowadays, "wreath symbolism" and "Love Conquers All" work fine together.

The colors of the flag

Jean Cioe also sent me a photo of a stool/storage bin decorated by John L. Smith. The symmetrical design is quite festive and it's painted with confident brush strokes. These might be the same tones of blue and gold he used for the flag design.

(See color version on the back cover of this book.)

THE NEWPORT CITY FLAG
IN THE 2000S

From the 1970s through the early 2000s, Leo Waring, and then Bert Duguay, of the Ebenezer Flagg Company on Spring Street sold Newport City Flags.

Unfortunately, that business closed its doors a few years ago.

In the year 2012, G. Brian Sullivan teamed up with artist and author Peter Tyler to recreate and deliver flags to help fan the flames of interest.

They managed to get large Newport City Flags flown at City Hall, Long Wharf, Touro Park, and in the Bellevue Plaza Shopping Center.

Soon, smaller versions of the flag started appearing on houses in the City by the Sea.

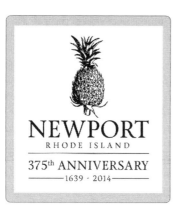

Newport's 375th Anniversary Parade in 2014

In 2014, "Newport's 375th Anniversary Celebration Committee" held a grand parade from One-Mile Corner, down Broadway, to the reviewing stand in Washington Square.

G. Brian Sullivan organized the Newport City Flag Marching Company to promote pride in the 84-year-old Newport City Flag.

The Marching Company was led by eight cadets from the Rogers High School JROTC, under the leadership of Colonel Carl W. Cowan.

Led by Mike Kowalczyk of Newport Pedicab, a fleet of 7 flag-adorned bike-chariots performed complex choreographic maneuvers.

YOU CAN BE A PART OF THE NEWPORT CITY FLAG REVIVAL

In the late 1920's, a lot of thought went into the design of the Newport City Flag. Two separate contests were held. The Flag Committee judges were some of the most well-respected artists and knowledgeable historians in Newport. They solicited the opinion of Howard M. Chapin, one of Rhode Island's greatest historians, and indeed, the fellow who literally "wrote the book" on Rhode Island seals and flags.

The flag went through a revision process in which the name Newport was deleted, and was replaced with a slogan that was used on this island back in 1641 for the proposed joint colony between Newport and Portsmouth called "Aquidneck." The motto these early colonists chose is a timeless expression that goes back 2000 years to Virgil.

Newport is steeped in history. But, over time, sometimes history gets lost. A flag that was so much a part of the Newport's should be used today, so it will be a part of the future.

No other city in America is a structure quite like the Old Stone Mill. And Newport would be hard-pressed to find a maxim more elegant than: "Love Shall Conquer All."

APPENDIX
(FOR SERIOUS SAILING ENTHUSIASTS)

Here are some more photos of 1930's America's Cup Challenge
from local newspapers and the November, 1930 *Yachting* magazine.

(Thanks to the Newport Public Library, the Redwood
Library, and the International Yacht Restoration
School's Museum of Yachting. Many articles come
from a scrapbook kept by Phil Crowther, Jr.)

NEWPORT MECCA FOR HUNDREDS OF VISITORS

City Transformed Into Great Crucible of Yachting World

Display of Luxurious Craft in
Harbor Greatest to Which City
Has Played Host

Crew of "Shamrock V" preparing for the start of the first race

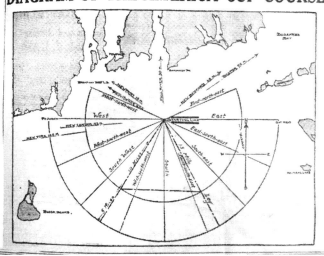

DIAGRAM OF THE AMERICA CUP COURSE

THE ENTERPRISE

Daily News
September 13, 1930

NEWPORT MECCA FOR HUNDREDS OF VISITORS

With an atmosphere of sentiment filled with the beautiful thought "They that go down to the sea in ships and do their business in great waters", the city of Newport is transferred from a quiet and peaceful isle of beauty and reat into the great crucible of the yachting world - - a crucible into which yachting devotees and enthusiasts were poured from all walks of life from early Friday morning until the time the official race between the Shamrock V, Sir Thomas Lipton's challenger, and the Enterprise, the defender of achievements and conquests of the Stars and Stripes in the yachting world, sailed to the point of starting this morning. Here in this port, where hundreds of vessels from all along the Atlantic coast sought anchorage Friday evening, presenting greatest display of luxurious craft to which the historic city has ever played host, the "Skeleton in Armor," immortalized by Longfellow, was brought to life.

Discussions and conversations on the wharves, in the boathouses, hotels, at street corners and in the byways and highways where men may wander in their idle moments, began with the present racing classic and drifted back to the days when the Viking ships skirted the coast of Newport and sought refuge in the harbor, to the time when the British and Americans engaged in warfare, to the advent of the French fleet, to the time when the city was the Mecca of the New World, including the day when the German submarine startled the nation by it's entrance into Narragansett Bay. Here, under the shadow of the Old Stone Mill and under the watchful eye of ancient Trinity, men talked with enthusiasm while they awaited the zero hour, and the ships that pass in the night were rocked on the quiet waves of the waters of Narragansett.

The harbor Friday evening was a thing of beauty, for the people of the city passed along the shore by hundreds, viewing the large fleet of yachts assembled. From the most luxurious craft to the little "putput" boats, the harbor was host to all. Searchlights played over the water from the Naval vessels. These piercing watchdogs of the night, as they were focussed now upon the sky, and now upon the fleet, presented a scene of beauty which will live long in memory. Every nook and corner of the harbor was occupied, and it was only with the greatest difficulty that the Commonwealth, chartered to carry hundreds of sightseers from various parts of New England and New York to view the races, managed to reach her dock this morning. The big vessel resembled the proverbial bull in the china shop, as she worked her way through the network of hundreds of yachts.

What the small boats carried in little quantities, the Commonwealth carried in bulk, for she was loaded with passengers for the big race. Like the Commonwealth was the Mount Hope, which made the turn of the Torpedo Station with decks black with people. The Jamestown boat, acting as a shuttle, brought hundreds over to the city this morning and the discharge from the 8 o'clock boat gave evidence of the "big parade", as they made their way to the small boats and big boats scheduled to visit the race course.

All morning long Thames Street was a channel of heavy traffic. Automobiles of every description rolled on their way, while taxis were forced to do some broken-field work in order to take their passengers to their appointed station at schedule time. Special officers were posted at various corners along the street, to aid in relieving congestion. The main street was bedecked with the colors of Great Britain and America dotted here and there with unique displays in the windows, of the races, Sir Thomas Lipton, and the history of the America's Cup. Everything was in tune for the international contest, and it is questionable whether any other port in the country could present the color, atmosphere and background that is Newport's by right of birth. As a result of the invitation extended by the Newport Yacht Club, welcoming all visiting yachtsmen to take advantage of the local quarters, the little club was an active place last night and today. Commodore E.V. Howe and former Commodore William M. Arnold were kept busy during the entire time, offering assistance to visitors. Boats arrived there from Boston, Taunton, Providence, New Bedford, and many small places along the Cape. The position of the Newport Club made it handy for those who stayed there as they were in the active section of the city, and a convenient distance from the theatre and shopping district.

Among the large number of yachts assembled in the harbor was that of Commodore E.J. Hartshorn of Canada. Mr. Hartshorn and party made the trip from the Dominion in the Migrace II, adding another group of enthusiasts to the already large number anxious to cheer for the victory of Shamrock V, Sir Thomas Lipton and the Royal Ulster Yacht Club.

One of the most interesting gatherings of Friday evening, was that of the newspapermen, many of whom had not shaken hands or chatted with one another for years. Warm associations were revived and the days of old were re-lived for another pleasant hour or more. As one hobnobbed about the lobbies of the hotels, where the men were gathered in little groups, some discussing the races, others recalling old times, and some breaking forth into song, one heard little stories about the World War, the A.E.F., and such expressions as "When I first saw Jim," "When we were together at-" and other remarks which spoke of pleasant memories. One man stated the whole thing to the point when he said this gathering of newspapermen was one of the greatest he had ever seen.

EXTRA
Daily News
September 13, 1930

.ENTERPRISE WINS FIRST RACE
IN DEFENSE OF AMERICA'S
CUP BY NEARLY
THREE MINUTES

The Enterprise made a long stride toward the successful defense of the America's Cup trophy, when she slid across the finish line 2 minutes 40 seconds ahead of the Shamrock V, Sir Thomas Lipton's challenger. Taking the lead at the start, when he directed his boat across the line a few seconds after the gun, Skipper Vanderbilt and his crew maintained a good lead over the English craft on the first leg, and on the homeward stretch managed to increase the distance between her and the green sloop.

The Enterprise crossed the finish line at 3:57:50, just 4 hours 2 minutes and 50 seconds from the start.

The Shamrock crossed the line at 4:00:30, 2 minutes and 40 seconds behind the defender.

The success of the Enterprise in the initial contest of the yachting classic of the world was due to the skillful and capable handling of the sloop by the skipper, Harold S. Vanderbilt, together with an equally skillful and capable crew. As in previous battles for the yachting supremacy of the world between America and England, it has been the superiority of the crew which has spelled the difference between success and failure. So it was today in the first contest. Throughout the entire race, the skipper of the "white ghost" outmaneuvered his rival, Ned Heard, the professional navigator whom Sir Thomas brought over with the hope that his skill and knowledge of yachting might prove a deciding factor in "bringing home the mug."

The sight presented at the races today was one of the greatest witnessed at an international classic. Every kind of boat was

LIPTON QUEST FILLS A ROYAL COMMAND

Challenges Have Cost Him $10,000,000 to Date—Humble Early Beginnings That Led to Road of Fortune

By ALLEN WILLIAM GROBIN

NEW YORK, Sept 13—A modern Sir Galahad in quest of a modern holy grail, Sir Thomas Lipton, like the knight of Arthurian legend, received his command from his king. For 32 years he has pursued the elusive America Cup, and now at 82 still hopes to win his quest before he dies.

His mission in search of the international yachting trophy had its origin in a casual suggestion of King Edward, then Prin...

"Something about me outside yachting? A great many will fancy that is like giving 'Hamlet' with the principal character left out, will they not?"

At 48 his fortune was estimated at $50,000,000, which he acquired through being among the first to apply the then new economic practice of concentration and collective buying.

A simple man, of the most appealing extrovert type, who translates achievement into terms of active doing, he finds his greatest relaxation in games of striving.

ENTERPRISE CREW ON WAY TO YACHT

Captain George Monsell (center) and the well-drilled crew of "Enterprise" handled the defender without a flaw

47

Photos by E. Levick

The first photographs made aboard the defender "Enterprise." Top, left: The boom which has caused so much comment. Right: The duralumin mast. Center: Looking forward below, "Enterprise" appears to be like a submarine. Bottom: One of the sail lockers, and transom and table under companionway, the only accommodations on board

Photos by E. Levick.

"Shamrock V" and the big spinnaker she carried in the light wind of the first race

wind she found herself beautifully covered by a green hull dead to windward of her. Vanderbilt waited about two minutes, and then as *Shamrock's* crew were flattening down the main sheet, slammed *Enterprise* about on to the port tack. *Shamrock* tried to cover her. But *Enterprise* was sailed with a rap full, right out from under the challenger, which seemed to lose a lot of headway in stays. As soon as he got his wind clear, Vander-

EXPECT LIGHT AIR FOR RACE TODAY

Enterprise-Shamrock Real Test In Second Tilt in Doubt— Visitors Undismayed

SIR THOMAS LIPTON ON THE ERIN, WATCHING THE SHAMROCK Far From Being Too Ill Declares, Stands Two Start Set Revenge In First Race.

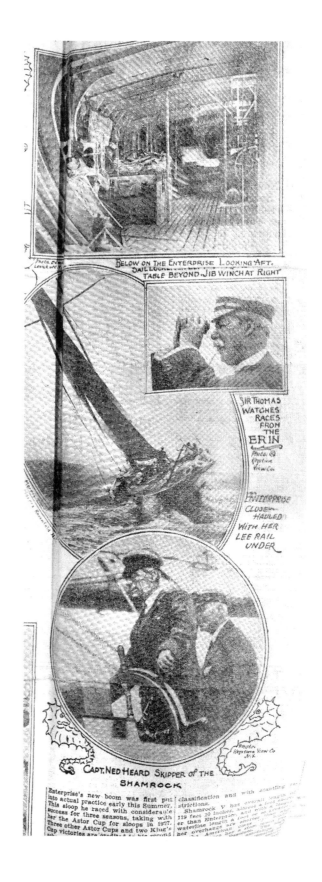

BELOW ON THE ENTERPRISE LOOKING AFT. SAILLOCKERS AT LEFT, TABLE BEYOND JIB WINCH AT RIGHT

SIR THOMAS WATCHES RACES FROM THE ERIN

ENTERPRISE CLOSE-HAULED WITH HER LEE RAIL UNDER

CAPT. NED HEARD SKIPPER OF THE SHAMROCK

Enterprise's new boom was first put into actual practice early this Summer. This sloop he raced with considerable success for three seasons, taking with her the Astor Cup for sloops in 1927. Three other Astor Cups and two King's Cup victories are credited to his record

classification and with sporting restrictions.

Shamrock V has overall measurements 119 feet 10 inches, almost a foot longer than Enterprise, and with a shorter waterline length. Her overhangs are longer and American

ENTERPRISE AFTER ROUNDING, SHAMROCK AT LEFT HEADING FOR MARK AT THE TURN

ENTERPRISE WINS FIRST RACE, GETTING JUMP

Leads From Start, Beating Shamrock Over 30-Mile Course by Margin Just Under Three Minutes, In Breeze Never Above Eight Knots

ENTERPRISE CROSSING FINISH LINE

Defender Boom Works Finely

Vanderbilt Scores as Skipper Test

Two Collisions, Damage Slight

$100,000,000 Parade in Day's Great Spectacle

ENTERPRISE BEATS SHAMROCK IN FIRST RACE

Enterprise, skippered by Harold S. Vanderbilt, is shown leading Sir Thomas Lipton's Shamrock V Saturday, during the first race of the American's cup series.

RACE 2

ENTERPRISE WINS SECOND RACE OF CUP SERIES

Associated Press Photo

Harold S. Vanderbilt's Enterprise, sailing a winning race all the way, scored its second straight victory over Sir Thomas Lipton's green Shamrock V in the classic yachting duel for the America's cup. Enterprise is shown right crossing the finish line. Above is the start of the race and picture below shows Enterprise leading the Shamrock V along the 30-mile triangular course.

Photos by M. Rosenfeld

Start of the third race. "Shamrock V" has "Enterprise" covered on the line. "Enterprise" tacks (center) and "Shamrock V" fails to come about at once. "Enterprise," with her wind clear, works up on challenger's lee bow and gets away. The difference in the way the main sheets of the two boats are trimmed is plainly shown

17th, to find a fine sou'wester of some 14-mile strength kicking up a fairly choppy sea over the 30-mile windward and leeward course. Just for a change, Captain Heard put it all over the *Enterprise* at the start. No attempt was made by either boat to cover the other. *Enterprise* went for the line on the starboard tack, but was too soon, and had to reach along it for several boat lengths. *Shamrock*, on the other hand, was almost perfectly timed, hitting the line on the starboard tack close to the committee tug. When *Enterprise* hauled up on the

seemed to work, for the green boat continued to gain on the Yankee craft. Half way home *Enterprise* set her Genoa jib, the wind having lightened somewhat. *Shamrock* set a bigger jib topsail, and carried this sail, plus a jib and the balloon foresail, to the finish. But as the wind hauled westerly, *Enterprise* set a spinnaker, and with this sail and her Genoa jib drawing beautifully, was drawing away from the Irish craft at the finish. But although she won by a margin of 5 minutes and 44 seconds, *Enterprise* had lost nearly 3 minutes on this last leg of the race and the series — the best showing *Shamrock* had made at any time during the match, but not nearly enough to offset the fearful drubbing which she had taken on the weather leg.

Harold S. Vanderbilt at the wheel of "Enterprise"

When "Shamrock's" main halliards "let go" in the third race

Watching the Pride of His Life
Sir Thomas Lipton, aboard his Erin, admires Shamrock V as she takes the water in racing trim. Left — Two sailors atop Shamrock V's mast, conditioning her.

Owner of the Challenger
Sir Thomas Lipton aboard his steam yacht Erin photographed while he was following the losing course of his Shamrock V in the second race.

SHAMROCK LOSES RACE WHEN DISABLED

Associated Press Photo

A broken halyard which let her huge mainsail fall to the deck put the Shamrock V out of the race against the Enterprise in the third of the series for the America's cup. The picture shows the Shamrock just after her canvas had collapsed with Enterprise sliding by to her third triumph.

RACE 4

YACHTING

Volume XLVIII   OCTOBER · 1930   Number IV

"Enterprise" slipping across the finish line in the last race, winner of the fourteenth match for the America's Cup

"Enterprise" Wins Fourteenth America's Cup Match

Photos by E. Levick

"Enterprise" on starboard tack, crossing "Shamrock V" soon after start of last race

Enterprise rounded the mark with a lead of over two minutes, and hardened sheets on the starboard tack for a close fetch for the finish, the shift in wind having turned the windward leg into a close reach. There seemed very little difference in the speed of the two boats for quite a time, but gradually *Enterprise* lengthened the gap, a length at a time. *Shamrock* was being pinched; *Enterprise* was driven hard full in the light going.

ENTERPRISE WINNING FINAL RACE AND SERIES

The Vanderbilt sloop is seen passing the tugboat at the finish line, with the American flag seeming to hail her successful defence of the America's cup.

was Lipton's direct statement to a Daily News reporter on board Erin Saturday afternoon, during the course of the reception which followed the presentation of the silver replica of the Old Stone Mill. In his speech of acceptance, Sir Thomas, among other things, said, "I hope to race again here before very long, if it can possibly be arranged." This statement led to a request for an amplification, with the result that a new challenge apparently is in the making.

VIEW OF NEWPORT HARBOR SHOWING YACHTS VALUED IN MILLIONS
ASSEMBLED FOR CUP RACES BETWEEN ENTERPRISE AND SHAMROCK

(Photograph by Charles McCormick of Globe Staff)

THE PICTURE WAS TAKEN FROM MARION EPPLEY'S ESTATE OVERLOOKING THE HARBOR. THE SHAMROCK V AND ENTERPRISE ARE AT THEIR MOORINGS. THE PICTURE WAS TAKEN LOOKING TOWARD THE NEW YORK YACHT CLUB QUARTERS AND THE NEWPORT TRAINING STATION

Saturday, when fog shrouded the course   "Shamrock, unless Skipper   "If we are to have a

FLEET OF PLEASURE CRAFT FOLLOWING THE
OPENING RACE OF AMERICA CUP SERIES

PART OF THE FLEET FOLLOWING FIRST AMERICA'S CUP RACE
Note Sir Thomas Lipton's *Erin* in centre and bad visibility.

The sightseeing fleet was the largest ever seen at an international race, but was well controlled by the efficient Coast Guard patrol

PRESENTED A NEW PHILCO RADIO

SIR THOMAS LIPTON AND MAYOR SULLIVAN, WITH THE INSTRUMENT, ON BOARD THE ERIN

NEWPORT'S DISTINGUISHED GUEST

SIR THOMAS LIPTON, as he appeared on his only visit to the city.
By Daily News Photographer.

119

SIR THOMAS OVERCOME AS HE ACCEPTS CUP

Felt Fine, However, as He Left N Y City Hall After Receiving Good-Will Token

NEW YORK, Dec 4 (A. P.)—Sir Thomas Lipton was presented a cup for his sportsmanship today, but in the middle of his address accepting it, he was overcome by the heat in the presentation chamber at City Hall and swayed into his chair without finishing.

"Unfortunately," he apologized as he was assisted to his seat, "I can't read as well as I used to." The rest of his address was read for him.

The "cup of good will," for which thousands of Americans subscribed so he might have a token of America's good will in lieu of the America's Yachting Cup which he has tried so vainly to win with his Shamrock vessels, was presented in the Aldermanic Chamber at City Hall by Mayor James J. Walker, who, with the humorist, Will Rogers arranged the public subscription for the cup.

Sir Thomas began his speech of acceptance by saying, "I have never had a higher honor paid me in th...

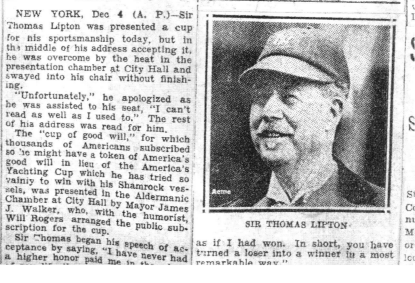

SIR THOMAS LIPTON.

as if I had won. In short, you have turned a loser into a winner in a most remarkable way."

SIR TOM SAYS HE'LL TRY AGAIN

Associated Press Photo

Undaunted after five failures to take back to Britain the International yachting trophy, Sir Thomas Lipton declared he would challenge again for the America's cup. He is shown (center) leaving New York city hall after a call on Mayor James Walker before sailing back to England.

SHAMROCK V AS SHE STRUGGLED TO REACH HOME.

on Her Eventful Return Voyage to England, Diving Into a Sea That Smothered Her Bows and Swept Her Deck.

120

After the races. Harold S. Vanderbilt wrote a book entitled:
Enterprise: The Story of the Defense of the America's Cup in 1930:

ENTERPRISE

The Story of the Defense of
The America's Cup
in 1930

By

HAROLD S. VANDERBILT

Chapter XV

THE RACES FOR THE AMERICA'S CUP, SEPTEMBER 13–18

Weather conditions on Saturday morning, September 13, were anything but auspicious. There was no wind, it was distinctly hazy, almost foggy, the sky was overcast and gray, and it looked as if it might rain at any moment. There was every indication that it would be impossible to start a race or to finish one within the time limit.

Newport harbor was literally alive with boats. In all its history such a fleet had never been assembled there. There were boats of every kind and description, and from all parts of the country. Large yachts, small yachts, Diesel yachts, auxiliary sailing yachts, power boats, house boats, motor launches. The smaller ones filled the inner harbor and Brenton Cove to capacity, the larger ones and several big excursion steamers from New York and Boston were anchored outside Goat Island. Farther up the bay, a Coast Guard fleet consisting of eight or ten revenue cutters, a number of destroyers and countless smaller craft was assembled. It was its duty to patrol the course and keep it clear for the contestants.

The Coast Guard issued explicit printed orders and directions to all boats attending the races. The orders required the sightseeing fleet to keep outside the patrol lines, and explained the manœuvres which the Coast Guard and its flock would execute. One set of evolutions was prescribed for a windward and leeward race, another for a triangular race. The instructions had been carefully prepared and the

194

TWO MINUTES AFTER THE START OF THIRD AMERICA'S CUP RACE

Enterprise (right) has not succeeded in sailing through *Shamrock V's* lee and is about to be blanketed by *Shamrock V. Enterprise* is about to tack (her crew are just springing into action), while the crew of *Shamrock V* are busy trimming main sheet

"SHAMROCK V" ON THE WIND

The camera is slightly on her lee bow. The luff of the jib topsail is sagging off to leeward badly and the jib somewhat, whereas the luff of the staysail is standing fairly straight. The actual sag is greater than that shown in the photograph, owing to the favourable angle at which it is taken. Note sag of *Shamrock V's* jib in photograph on page 2085.

isfied, we wonder, with the performance of the yacht of their choosing? Surely our victories over *Shamrock V* have vindicated our selection, if any vindication is needed.

And *Shamrock V,* where is she? We look astern. She is about a mile behind, a badly beaten boat; not only in this race but in all the others, except possibly the first. Our hour of triumph, our hour of victory, is all but at hand, but it is so tempered with sadness that it is almost hollow. To win The America's Cup is glory enough for any yachtsmen, why should we be verging on the disconsolate?

Uppermost in our minds is a feeling of sympathy for that grand old sportsman, Sir Thomas Lipton, with whom our relations have been so pleasant. This is perhaps his last attempt, it will soon prove a futile one, to lift The America's Cup. The ambition of a lifetime, to achieve which he has spent millions, is perhaps never to be realized. It has been our duty to shut the door in his face. We picture him

210

From a photograph by Morris Rosenfeld

TEN SECONDS AFTER THE START OF SECOND AMERICA'S CUP RACE

The photograph was taken from the Race Committee tug. The starting buoy at other end of line is visible under the after end of *Enterprise's* reaching main boom. *Shamrock V,* which has not yet crossed the line, is luffing to trim the main sheet, on which the man at left of photograph is hauling.

202

BETWEEN FRIENDS

THE AMERICAN SPORTSMAN.—If we can not keep both, I would rather lose the cup than lose you, Sir Thomas.

The caption of this double-page spread illustration in the 1930 *Puck* magazine reads:

"BETWEEN FRIENDS

An American Sportsman: If we can not keep both,
I would rather lose the cup than lose you, Sir Thomas."

(Yes, even competitive gentlemen realize, "Love Shall Conquer All.")

Made in the USA
Middletown, DE
17 June 2017

Tactical Strongman